SUPERPUPPY

HOW TO CHOOSE, RAISE, AND TRAIN THE BEST POSSIBLE DOG FOR YOU

BY JILL AND D. MANUS PINKWATER

Line drawings by Jill Pinkwater

A Clarion Book

The Seabury Press · New York

Second Printing

The Seabury Press, 815 Second Avenue, New York, New York 10017

Text copyright © 1977 by Jill and D. Manus Pinkwater
Illustrations copyright © 1977 by Jill Pinkwater
Designed by Barbara Hall
Printed in the United States of America.

Library of Congress Cataloging in Publication Data
Pinkwater, Jill.
    Superpuppy: how to choose, raise, and train the best possible dog
for you.
    "A Clarion book."
    Includes index.
    SUMMARY: A guide to buying, training, and caring for a dog, with
special emphasis on understanding its personality, feelings, and
reactions to new situations.
    1. Dogs—Juvenile literature. [1. Dogs] I. Pinkwater, D. Manus,
joint author. II. Title.
SF426.5.P56   636.7   76-8825
ISBN 0-8164-3176-0

To Juno and Arnold
—who have been very patient with us.

ACKNOWLEDGMENTS

We wish to give special thanks to: Oscar, Potemko, Bear, Wakame, Living Skunk, Dead Skunk, Herm David (especially for suggesting the "How to Find a Lost Dog" chapter), Quanah, Daisy's Puppy, Red Puppy, Arnoldine, Ranger, No-name, Tonka, Kaleb, Eric, King, Doc, Baron, Rascal, Max, Argyle, Phil Euler, Layla, Queenie, Sparky, Fifty, Christine, Shasta, Dr. Figarola, Rebel, Butch, Péle, Barkley, Dr. Golden, Brett, Pudgy, Keema, Choo-choo, Peaches, Dr. Bleibtreu, Jolly Roger, Blue Jet, Snowball, Patty-cake, Tabby, Sundown, Happy, Chace, Boris, Leo, Cocquette, Doodle, Shep, Fafner, Urrf, Gretel, Heidi, Duchess, Klutz, Jason, Sno Wolf, Sno Wolf Jr., Nikki, Queenie, Eric the Red, Charley, Ziggy, Siddhartha, Bracchus, Cherry, Frosty, Kelly, Whiskers, Lance, Bambi, Sam, Kojac, Oyuki, Pippa, Stormy, Barney, Dr. Vanderbilt, Belle, Kerry, Bootsie, Tripod, Blackie, Penny, Nelly, Brandy, Moses, Daisy, Banana, Cutie, Ho, Pet, Pal, Bridget, Shane, Jolly, Buffalo Bill, and all the others whose names we don't remember.

CONTENTS

INTRODUCTION

Imagine that soon after you were born, as soon as you were able to live away from your mother, you were tossed into a cage, and left there for a few years. Someone would bring you food and clean up your mess every day, but you would have nothing to do, nothing to see, nowhere to go. You would never get any exercise, never make any friends, never go to school, never learn to read, never know that anyone loved you. What sort of person would you be if all those things had happened to you? Would you still be you? How much of you is the result of things you've learned, not just in school, but every minute of your life?

Of course, nothing like that happened to you; if it had you certainly wouldn't be reading this book. You were taken care of, loved, fed, taught, and given the chance to learn things for yourself. That is part of the reason you are the kind of person you are today.

This is a book about dogs. Like you, a dog has a personality. And like yours, the dog's personality is a combination of whatever the dog was at the moment it was born, and whatever has happened to it since.

In general, people have a good idea of how to take care of young children, but lots of dogs are not taken care of lovingly when they need it most. They wait in cages, doing nothing through some of the most important weeks of their lives, and are taken to live with people who expect their new puppy to grow up to be a terrific pet without any help at all. When the puppy doesn't work out, these people are disappointed. They blame the dog for not trying to fit in. They may give the dog away, or sometimes they call a dog trainer when problems become enormous. Often the trainer can help, but how much better it would have been if the dog had been trained before he was a mass of bad habits! Lots of dogs do work out without any special help; they stop eliminating all over the house at an early age; they don't chew up the good furniture; they don't wake everybody up in the middle of the night; they don't climb all over visitors—they are good, smart dogs. They could have been wonderful, brilliant dogs with a little help!

There is a lot of fun and satisfaction in living with dogs, and a lot of work and responsibility. All puppies start out about even. Whether they turn out to be wonderful or ordinary depends on what happens to them, and most of what happens to them depends on people—on you.

The authors of this book don't know everything about dogs; nobody does. We don't guarantee that if you read this book you are going to wind up living with a Lassie. What we hope to do is give you some basic information which you can combine with your own common sense. You must make the decision whether to have a dog, how to pick the right one, and how to take care of your dog. And you have to help that dog to become something extra special.

We hope that you have been given lots of opportunities to grow and learn and be the best kind of person possible. We hope you appreciate all the things that have combined to make you the very special person you are, and we hope this book will help you to understand your dog, and help the puppy grow into a wonderful friend. Your dog wants to be that and you deserve it too.

SUPERPUPPY

1. DO YOU WANT A DOG?

Do you want a dog? What are they good for? Why does anyone keep a dog in the first place? Dogs have to be fed, trained, and taken to the vet. They demand attention. Even with the best of advice, the puppy who is guaranteed never to mess up the house, or eat a library book or your good shoes, hasn't been born yet. What's the point of living with one?

Dogs and people have been living together for a long time. Nobody knows for sure when the first wild ancestor of the dog moved in with the first wild ancestor of ours, and we can only guess what the dog and man had in mind. Most people believe that dog and man went into a hunting partnership—the dogs finding and chasing game, and the men sharing part of the kill with them. Somewhere along the way, the two became friends as well as partners.

In some places, dogs still work for a living. Dogs still hunt with men (for sport, not survival). Dogs herd sheep and cattle, pull sleds and wagons, track and rescue lost persons, patrol and guard property, sniff out contraband and narcotics, perform in circuses and the show ring, and guide blind persons.

You might have an idea that it would be fun or useful to teach your dog to do some kind of work, but that's hardly the reason most people get started living with one. Most dogs who live with people

Working dogs

today are pets. They are there for the pleasure of the people they live with.

Unfortunately, some dogs are ornaments—people buy them because they think a dog will look good lying in front of the fireplace. Some dogs are ornaments for their owner's reputation—they travel to dog shows with hired professional handlers. These dogs almost never live at home; the owners have photographs, and a bunch of blue ribbons. Some people buy dogs to intimidate or attack other people; some people buy dogs as toys, play with them for a while, and then ignore them or give them away, or turn them loose. We don't approve of these people, but we do feel sorry for their dogs.

Most people, we are happy to report, have a much better reason for wanting a dog; they want to share love with the dog. They want a loving nonhuman friend. They are responding to that feeling the first prehistoric man must have had when he invited a puppy to share his cave. There's something very nice about having a friend who isn't another human being; it makes us feel closer and more in harmony with all of creation. A dog makes a unique kind of friend, one which is uncritical, ever-forgiving, loyal, and completely devoted to you. When you forget yourself, and do something intolerant or selfish (and we all do), the dog is always ready to forget about it and start over.

Besides being a good moral influence, dogs have personalities. They have likes and dislikes, moods and enthusiasms very much as we do.

When a dog comes to live with a family, that family becomes larger by one member. Most dogs are nice and aren't hard to get along with. But *really* getting along with a dog, coming to a special understanding with one, is something else. One of the authors remembers sitting on a rock overlooking a river with his dog and realizing, for the first time, that he and the dog were both thinking the same thought. Nothing complicated, just something like, "Ah! What a nice day." It was thrilling to know that this was really *his* dog, that he had a private understanding with her that neither of them had with anyone else in the world.

Besides being a potential friend, dogs are members of a foreign species, more foreign than any person from another country. Dogs have their own kind of social behavior, very different from ours, but close enough that we can learn quite a lot about it. Dogs have language of a sort; we can learn what their facial expressions and body language mean, and they can (and do) learn ours, as well as learning some of our spoken language. If you've ever had the thought that it would be exciting to be the first person to meet and try to communicate with a man from outer space, then you might derive a lot of pleasure from learning the language, social rules, and courtesies of dogs. Your dog will be happy to teach you.

The authors have dogs and cats. Some people love dogs and can't see the point of cats. Some people love cats and hate dogs. We like reptiles, read books about them, look at them in the zoo, aren't scared of snakes, but don't keep reptiles as pets. We just don't like them in that way. Some people keep reptiles as pets, and get a lot of pleasure from them. What we're trying to say is that not everybody wants a dog, nor *should* everybody want one. It doesn't mean that there's something wrong with you if you don't feel like having a dog; and it doesn't mean that you're necessarily going to miss something important in life if you never have one. If you are meant to be a dog-owning person, then one way or another, you're going to own dogs, and enjoy them and learn from them—if not now, then later on. If you are not a dog-owning person, you are going to find more work than pleasure in owning one.

If you are reading this book in preparation for owning a dog, this might be a good time to do some thinking about whether you really want a dog, and just what you expect owning a dog to be like. Let your imagination run a little. Our experience has been that the more developed one's expectations are, the easier it is to accomplish something which comes close to those expectations—within limits. If you want to train your dog like Lassie, there isn't a reason in the world why you can't, but it isn't going to happen the first week. Expectation seems to count, especially with dogs. When people bring their dogs to our school, the dogs almost always work better for us than for their own people. It isn't because we are magic, and it isn't

What you expect is what you get

because we are doing anything we don't tell the people about. It's just that we fully expect the dog to listen, and do as he's told—so he does. This is something for the whole family to consider. If everyone has agreed that the family will have a dog, and one person keeps saying, "I just know the puppy is going to be impossible, chew up the furniture, dump on the rug," you'd better have some more family conversations before you get the dog. We can't really tell why this is, but somehow dogs almost always fulfill your expectations. By the same token, if you expect the new puppy to be a lot of fun and almost no trouble at all, with a little help from you, he'll be just that.

Do some more imagining; is the dog someone you look forward to knowing, or is it just the idea of the dog you like? We meet people in our school who have a dog, but really wanted a little furry human being. "He just won't *listen* to us," they say about an eight-week-old puppy. Others want the dog to be something they're not—tough or aristocratic, for instance. Men have come in with cute little German Shepherd puppies and talk about their dogs as dangerous man killers. We see lots of pretty girls who have long flowing honey-colored hair with Afghan Hounds with long flowing honey-colored hair. We can't help wondering if those girls are going to get another dog if they dye their hair another color. Don't get a dog to make you look good! Don't get a dog to bolster up your ego! Don't get a dog as a substitute for a human child! Dogs have a lot of talent for being dogs; if you give them a chance, they can be surprisingly good at it.

Before you decide whether you are a dog-owning person or not, do a lot of visiting. Visit friends who have dogs, and use the opportunity to spend a little time with their dogs. If a friend will lend you a dog for a day or two, you can find out a lot about how you might get along with one of your own. Every dog is different so make a few experiments, not just one.

There's no hurry; there are lots of dogs around to choose from. You have plenty of time to find out things that will enable you to pick the puppy that's right for you.

2. THE DOG AND THE FAMILY

As much as you may want a dog, you should know that a dog does not fit into every family. This means families of one as well as families of six or more. Before you arrive home one day with a cute puppy, consider your family carefully. If there is more than one person living in a household, then the decision to get a dog must involve every family member, even those too small to participate in the discussion. If you do this, you will be on the way to making a good decision, and will probably be able to overcome objections to a puppy with intelligent arguments.

A dog may have a lot to offer your family. Raised with love and care, a puppy can become a wonderful dog. If you, or members of your family expect more (or less) you're in for trouble. It isn't a burglar alarm, a toy, a symbol of status like a mink coat. It is a dog. If you and your family have decided that you like dogs, and would enjoy having one around, whether he turns out to be useful and bright or a companionable idiot, you may be rewarded by years of the best kind of friendship.

WITH WHOM DO YOU LIVE? Before getting a dog you must take into account every family member. First of all, how big is your family? A tiny dog tends to get lost underfoot in a large family. A giant dog in a large family is sometimes too expensive to feed. How old are your family members? Some dogs are gentler with children than others. Some small children are too rough for certain breeds. Do you have a grandparent, or other older person, living with you who will be walking the dog some of the time? Some breeds are difficult to train and too rough for some older people, or people not in robust health.

What is your family schedule? Will there be someone at home with the puppy during the day? It is possible to raise a puppy in a home where the adults work and the children are at school, but certain problems, such as destructiveness and housebreaking, will be much more difficult to solve. If the family is at work and school from 8 A.M. to 5 P.M., and sleeps from 11 P.M. to 7 A.M., that leaves the dog with *seven* hours of company per day. If you keep a dog under those conditions, you owe him *all* seven hours. Maybe it would be better to wait for a time when you can devote more hours to the dog. Also consider getting a pet for the dog, a kitten, a parakeet; dogs don't enjoy being alone.

If no one really has time for the puppy or dog, time to brush it, walk it, play with it, take it to the veterinarian, then maybe you should look into tropical fish instead. Every dog needs attention beyond feeding and walking.

If the mother of the family is the only one who is home all day, she will be doing much of the work involving a puppy. Even if the dog officially belongs to somebody else, it will be Mom who spends her day with it. If she also has one or more small children to look after, it might be rough dealing with an energetic young puppy. We have known some nice families who had to give up nice puppies because the mother of young children found that a puppy was more work than she could handle. If this is a possibility in your family, it may be better to wait.

Does everyone in your family want a dog? Is anyone afraid of dogs or afraid of a certain kind of dog? One dissatisfied family member can ruin a puppy's chances for a lifetime home. A young sister or brother who is rough on a puppy or very jealous of a puppy can provoke the gentlest dog into nipping. A child as young as three or four can do terrible damage to a very young puppy. Most children won't do this, but many have to be taught how to hold and play with an animal. Who in the family will do this teaching?

WHOSE DOG WILL IT BE? Everyone in the family may love the new puppy, but one person must take responsibility for the dog. There should be one person who keeps a record of the puppy's shots, worm checks and general health. One person should be responsible for making sure the dog is brushed, bathed and checked for ticks and fleas. One person should be responsible for checking the dog's ears and nails, cleaning and clipping, feeding, walking on schedule, and training. If most or all of these responsibilities fall on the person who didn't really want the dog in the first place, the dog may not be in your family for long.

OVERCOMING OBJECTIONS: If you really want a dog and one or more of your family is against the idea, or perhaps skeptical, you may be able to overcome objections with intelligent arguments. Never surprise your family with a puppy before you have overcome the objections. You may have fallen in love with the animal, but the first time the pup makes a mistake and piddles on the carpet, the dog may be on its way to the pound.

Here is how to build your case. Let your family know that you have decided to make time to care for the puppy. Be sure you really have the time. If it happens that you are simply between activities, make sure that you will have time to give the dog when your life gets busy again. Do some research regarding dogs. Get books out of the library, and find a breed or type that will fit into your family.

It is impossible for us to give an accurate idea of exactly how much it costs to buy and maintain a dog. By the time this book is published, prices will have changed. Also, things have different costs in different areas. It might be wise to contact a few local veterinarians and find out what they charge for an office visit, for shots, for neutering. Find out what quantities of food are recommended for specific breeds you are considering and how much that feeding will cost day after day and year after year. Are you considering a breed that will require the services of a professional groomer? How much do they charge? How often does the dog have to go? Will you be needing a professional dog trainer or obedience class? How much is charged for these services where you live? And finally, how much does the dog, itself, cost? Some rare breeds sell for hundreds of dollars and a mutt from the pound might only cost the price of a license.

Everyone in the family should be involved in making the decision to have a dog or not. In gathering information about the pros and cons you will be helping yourself as well as your family to decide if you really want one. We have known cases in which only one person in the family wanted a dog and by the time all the research was done, the whole family was unanimous in wanting one. We have also known cases in which the whole family started out wanting a dog and wound up with a couple of goldfish once they knew all the facts.

3. WHERE DO YOU LIVE?

In addition to considering all of the people you live with, you must consider the location and size of your home before you decide to buy a dog. Some dogs shed a lot, some need extra amounts of exercise, some are too big for some spaces.

HOUSING: How big is your home? Is it a small apartment, a house with a yard, a country house with lots of land? Is it crowded with people and things? There probably isn't a human residence on earth where some dog would not be happy. People can even keep huge, energetic dogs in tiny apartments if special arrangements are made to give the dog needed exercise. Still, it makes sense to try to match the dog to your living conditions. Space is an important consideration in choosing the right dog; healthy puppies are active, and are going to spend some of their time racing through the rooms of your home. Puppies are fairly small, but a six-month-old Great Dane, or Alaskan Malamute or Collie full of pep and energy can seem twice as big as it actually is.

Another consideration is what floor you live on. If you live in an apartment, how many flights up? Who will be walking the puppy? If you live on the fourth floor, who is going to go up and down the stairs many times a day? (Someone will have to.) Even after the housebreaking is finished, and the pup is on a regular schedule, someone will have to walk those steps with the dog at least four times a day for the dog's life. If you live in a high-rise apartment building, on what floor are you? If you live on the twelfth or fifteenth floor, going up and down in the elevator will take time. Do you have the time, especially in the morning, to make the trip with a puppy or dog? If you do it right, the dog will never make a mistake in the elevator—but if you make a mistake, he may. Are you prepared to clean it up? Some people who have terraces attached to their apartments let the dogs use the terrace as a toilet. They're sorry later, when they take the dog on a trip, and there isn't a terrace for him to use.

None of the above considerations makes it impossible to have a dog. We simply feel that you ought to do some thinking along these lines. Discuss it with your family.

LOCALE: The breed you wind up with will have certain special requirements and characteristics. We don't feel that it is necessarily cruel to keep an Irish Setter, for example, in a city apartment. But it is your responsibility to see that the dog has a *good* workout every day. If you jog a mile a day, a Setter might be fine. He'll jog with you. There are many other breeds which need running space and a workout several times a week (not just on Sunday)! There are also breeds which require somewhat less exercise (although all dogs need *some*) and a number of toy breeds can get their quota of exercise by racing around an apartment.

So consider where you live before selecting a puppy. Do you live in a large urban center? Do you live in the suburbs or in a rural location? Are there parks nearby where you can run the dog? What are the local leash laws concerning dogs? Are they allowed in the parks? Call the police station or city hall to check on the regulations in your area. There may be a wonderful park with fields three blocks from your home, and a local law prohibiting dogs off leash— or dogs at all.

You must also consider where you can walk your dog for the purpose of elimination. Check local laws regarding dog stool. More and more towns and cities are requiring owners to clean up after their dogs.

AUTOMOBILES: Does your family have a car? If it doesn't, are you within walking distance of a veterinarian? Can you afford to call a taxi to take you to the vet for the necessary treatment the puppy will need? Is there a car that can be borrowed for this purpose? Very small dogs can sometimes be put into carriers and taken onto buses, trains, and subways. Medium and large-sized dogs present more of a problem.

If your family has a car, how big is it? Is there room in the car for your family and a grown dog? How large a dog? You can squeeze a Mastiff into a Volkswagen, but it will not be very comfortable, and there won't be much room for you.

INDOOR AND OUTDOOR DOGS: Are you planning to have an indoor or outdoor dog? Some people want their dogs to live in a yard with a doghouse. This is not our favorite approach to dog ownership—one misses much pleasure by not living *with* the dog. But there seem to be many perfectly happy yard dogs around. If your family has decided to keep the dog in the yard, you must again consider the breed you are going to buy. If you live in a very warm or very cold climate, some dogs will not do well out of doors all the time. For example, a short-haired hound would be fine in South Carolina, but miserable, or even sick if kept outside through a Maine winter. A Siberian Husky would love the Maine winter but might suffer during a Florida summer spent out of doors, unless special attention were paid to providing shade and water for the dog.

SHEDDING: All dogs shed hair. There is no way to totally avoid dog hair if you own a dog. If you live in a very formal house, you might prefer a breed which sheds very little (Poodles) or sheds seasonally (northern breeds). Brushing several times a week certainly helps the shedding problem, as does a good healthful diet. But unless you buy a Mexican Hairless dog, there will be shedding. Despite appearances, dogs with short stiff coats will shed as much as dogs with longer silkier coats. The longer coated dogs will need more grooming (brushing and combing) to keep out tangles and to remove burrs, twigs and mud, but the time spent on these jobs may be worth it to you and your family.

FEEDING AND CARE EXPENSE: Every dog costs money to keep, especially if it gets the right kind of veterinary care. However, larger dogs can get to be much more expensive to feed. Can your family afford to feed a large dog? The giant breeds eat giant quantities of food. Some breeds can go through five or six pounds of food a day.

If your family tends to go on vacation where a dog will not be welcome, or where a dog simply cannot go, you must consider the cost of boarding. People who board dogs usually charge in relation to a dog's size.

NEIGHBORS: Another thing to consider in choosing the right kind of dog for your family is your neighbors. Do you share a common yard with anyone? Will they object to your having a dog? Do your neighbors have a dog? Is it apt to be friendly, or will you have to keep your new puppy away from it? Most dog neighbors learn to get along, but it might be a good idea to find out the dog-next-door's record with other dogs. Will barking disturb any of your neighbors? There are breeds of dog which bark less than other breeds. There is even one that does not bark at all (Basenji). Terriers are known for their love of making a racket. If you consider these things, and consult with your neighbors before you bring the puppy home, you might avoid a feud.

4. TYPES OF DOGS

What's available? We've all seen Poodles and German Shepherds but what other kinds of dogs are there? What are the differences between breeds? There are well over a hundred different breeds of dog in this country (we don't know how many worldwide) and there are mongrels, combinations of any number of breeds.

Every purebred dog, and every mongrel, has a special personality. There are certain things that dogs of a particular breed may have in common, but there are always greater differences between individuals within breeds than between breeds. Some trainers will say, "A German Shepherd is apt to behave like this" or "an Airedale is apt to behave like that." We take this kind of folklore into account, but we try not to generalize. We have seen so many exceptions to the accepted ideas about breeds, that we don't assume a dog is going to behave or respond in any special way just because he belongs to a particular breed.

CHARACTERISTICS: There are some general observations we can make. For example, a Great Dane is certainly going to be larger than a Chihuahua. Also, certain categories of dogs have been bred over the years for a specific purpose, and this will affect their physical and nervous structure, personality, and responses. But please keep in mind that what happens to a dog after he's born is far more important than what breed he happens to be.

Dogs are huge, tiny, shaggy, smooth, graceful and lumbering, handsome and comical. As far as we know they all have the same ancestors, an unlovable creature called Miacis some forty million years ago, and more recently, the wolf. It may be hard to imagine a Poodle or a Cocker Spaniel having a wolf for a remote grandfather, but that is what the best evidence suggests to scientists. Dogs in different parts of the world evolved differently, in the same way that humans of different races look slightly different. We instantly recognize other humans as human; likewise dogs instantly recognize one another as dogs. All dogs are intrafertile—that means they can mate with any other dog (this includes wolves and coyotes) and produce true dog puppies, who can in turn reproduce.

We said that dogs in different places evolved with slight differences, but if you have looked at a picture book of dog breeds, you will have noticed that the differences aren't so slight. At first glance it's hard to find much in common between a Pekingese and a Saint Bernard. This simply points up another element in the natural history of dogs—man. A million or so years ago, dogs all probably looked pretty much alike, bigger, smaller, lighter, darker, smoother or shaggier, but clearly the same sort of animal. There was probably nothing as extreme as a Dachshund or a Bulldog. However, man took a hand in selecting qualities he liked or needed in a dog, and encouraged them to develop. He did this by selective breeding.

Let's say you want to have a dog who is good at going into holes to chase badgers. All the dogs around are sort of nondescript characters—a certain amount of variety, but nothing too extreme. Some of them enjoy chasing badgers down holes, some don't. You look around for a dog who is crazy about chasing badgers, and mate him with another dog who is built for it—let's say she has slightly shorter legs which are good for working in tunnels. The puppies are short-legged dogs who like to chase badgers. You breed the puppies, but only the shortest-legged, crazy-about-badger-chasing ones. You breed them to other dogs with characteristics you like, for example, a long snout, and flop ears that don't get full of dirt in badger holes. By now you've got a few families of dogs, covering a few generations, who tend to be short-legged-long-snouted-flop-eared-badger-chasers. You then breed only the short-legged-long-snouted-flop-eared-badger-chasers to other short-legged-long-snouted-flop-eared-

The making of
a short-legged-long-snouted-flop-eared-badger-chaser

badger-chasers. Of course, the puppies will very soon all turn out along the lines of the generations before them. Along the way, you can make some improvements; let's say you feel the legs could be even shorter. You do the same thing all over again, only this time you're concentrating on the legs, and you've got a whole lot of short-legged-long-snouted-flop-eared-badger-chasers to choose from. After a while you get tired of calling them short-legged-long-snouted-flop-eared-badger-chasers, and start calling them Dachshunds. You've created a breed.

Some breeds were created just like that, by one person in a relatively few years. The Doberman Pinscher was invented in the nineteenth century by a man named Dobermann. Other breeds have been created in a less deliberate manner. Some ten or fifteen thousand years ago the Eskimos found out that you could catch wolves and get them to pull sleds. They bred the best wolves, and ate the ones who didn't work out. Somewhere along the way a little mixture of domestic dog might have gotten mixed in. The Eskimos needed a dog with a speciality—strength. They didn't care too much what size the dog was, or if his ears flopped down or stood up. They just wanted a dog who would pull like crazy, and not eat too much. The dogs had to have warm coats so they could stand the cold, but the Eskimos probably didn't do any fancy long-range breeding. The dogs that were around were the ones suitable for the purpose; the best ones survived and reproduced. The authors live with a couple of sled dogs, and they aren't much different from the first photographs made of dogs Eskimos were using when the first man with a camera arrived. Chances are, they aren't much different from the dogs the Eskimos were using ten thousand years ago.

BREEDS: The American Kennel Club (the A.K.C.) somewhat arbitrarily divides purebred dogs into six groups: the Hound Group, Nonsporting Group, Sporting Group, Terriers, Toys, and Working Dogs. And there are mutts, of course. Look around for a picture book which describes the different breeds of dog. If it is a good one, it will tell a little about the history of the breed, give a good description of the sizes and colors available, and show a good picture of the dog. The picture book will tell something about the personality of the breed. Some of these books have the same thing to say about every dog—they are noble, dignified, loyal, brave, cheerful, trustworthy, and honest. That sort of information doesn't really tell you much about what it would be like to live with the dog.

Of course, everybody thinks that the breed he or she likes best is better than any other. If we tell you that Lhasa Apsos are tough cookies, and if there are small children in a family with one, there's apt to be trouble, we will get outraged letters from people who raise Lhasa Apsos and children, and everything is just fine. If we tell you that Irish Setters are big, good-natured slobs, we will have to forget that someone brought one to us last week who was a sneaky, biting, neurotic so-and-so. There is no such thing as an all-around dog, a breed that's good for everybody.

We don't suggest that you pick a breed just from looking in a breed book. Try to get to know some dogs. If you call the local newspaper, you may be able to find out where and when a fun match or puppy match (the A.K.C. calls them "sanctioned matches") will be held. This is where you can at least get an idea of what the different breeds of dog look like. A fun match is a practice dog show. Things

HOUND   SPORTING   NONSPORTING

TERRIER   TOY   WORKING

American Kennel Club purebred dog classifications

are more relaxed at a fun match, and people have time to talk and enjoy themselves (they ought to do the same at an official show, but some people are overly serious about winning).

So far this chapter hasn't really suggested what kind of dog you ought to get. And it isn't going to either. Recently we read a dog training book for young readers by a famous dog expert. He made a list of breeds that were especially suited for kids. On his list we found a few breeds that we have often experienced as very tricky to train—and he left out some obvious choices. How could this famous dog expert suggest some desperate characters as good dogs for young kids, and leave out such great, easy, lovable breeds? Is he some kind of fake? Of course not, and neither are we. The fact is that breeds are a matter of taste, choice, and luck. Whether a dog turns out to be good or bad has a lot more to do with how he's bred, chosen, raised, and trained, than what breed of dog he is.

We all have our favorites and un-favorites. The authors love Alaskan Malamutes, which most people agree are about the worst dogs for living with you can find; they're sneaky, muscle-bound clowns, they steal, and fight other dogs, and are never serious about anything. We love them, we're good at training them, we think their jokes (like throwing their master down a hill) are sort of funny. We don't like German Shepherds, which everybody knows are wonderful, intelligent, trainable dogs. The point is, there are plenty of people who would disagree with us—and they'd be right—and we're right too. You have to make up your own mind about a given breed of dog.

SOME WARNINGS: Here's one thing to look out for: The more popular a breed gets, the more people there will be who start breeding them without knowing what they're doing. Part of the reason we've hardly seen a good German Shepherd for years is that it is the second most popular breed in the country. If you decide that you want a dog whose breed is recently very popular, be ten times as careful! If you decide on a very rare breed, there's a different problem; you will be lucky to find one, and you have to take what you can get. If you write to the American Kennel Club (their address is in the back of this book), they will send you a list of breeds in order of the number registered. A good approach might be to pick from the middle third of the list. The A.K.C. will also send you a list of the national clubs which sponsor registered breeds. You can write to the clubs and ask for information about the breed, what the going price for a puppy is, where to find breeders.

Mutts have only one drawback: Unless you've seen the parents, you won't be able to tell what the dog will wind up looking like. He might be small, he might be a giant—you have to wait and see.

You can't tell much about a mixed-breed dog unless you've seen its parents; and you can't tell everything about a purebred puppy based solely on what sort of purebred it happens to be. We have said that differences between individuals are greater than differences between breeds, and suitability is more a matter of how the puppy is raised than what kind of dogs his parents were. There are some interesting and useful things you *can* find out about a particular breed. If you are interested in selecting a dog, and have a breed or two in mind, talk to some people who own that kind of dog, and don't talk to just one person, either! We have been to club matches where there were six hundred experts, all talking at once, and all convinced that the other 599 were wrong about everything. Dogs seem to bring out that kind of behavior. If somebody tells you that Chow Chows always bite the mailman, just file the information until you have heard it from five or six Chow Chow owners. If they all agree, and you still want a Chow Chow, maybe you will want to train the dog with emphasis on *not* biting the mailman.

BREED DIFFERENCES: There are differences between breeds and types of dogs that aren't especially important in selecting a dog to live with, but are interesting to learn about once you're living with the dog. Hounds are going to have keen sight or smell; bird dogs are very sensitive to birds; our Alaskan Malamutes can find something dead and nasty under two feet of snow and ice; we've been told that Mastiffs will stand across their master's body, and guard him if he lies on the ground; many sheep dogs have a natural talent for herding and managing and moving people, dogs, cats, and so on. Whether you use him for the purpose or not, you may enjoy seeing

the traces of the work your dog was originally bred for showing up in his behavior.

Differences between breeds that *are* important have to do with his size, need for activity, special problems, special features of temperament, lifespan, and so forth. These are things you have to do some serious research about. If you live in a city apartment, have a full schedule at school or work, are interested in a particular breed of dog, and then find out from responsible people who live with the breed that he *must* have a two-hour run every day, maybe you'd better look around for something else. Some dogs only live nine years or so; that is considered a drawback by many potential owners. Some breeds, notably hounds and certain herding dogs, have a smell that is more suitable to out of doors. Some long haired breeds need a daily grooming or they turn into a tangled knot. Some breeds are noisy, some breeds are nearly silent. Some breeds have been bred to be suspicious of strangers, some are everybody's pal. It is up to you to get an idea of what special features your breed has—and you may have to sort out some contradictory information.

MAKING THE FINAL DECISION: If you think you'd like to live with a Labrador Retriever, spend as much time as you can with Labrador Retrievers, at dog shows, fun matches, at the homes of people who own them, at kennels where they are raised. Don't pick out your breed from a picture book. We did that with our Malamutes, and it happened to work out. But we also had quite a few big surprises that the book didn't prepare us for. We were lucky. We remember a man who came to our school with a Hungarian Kuvasz, the only one he'd ever seen was the one he bought. He was discovering every day that his dog came complete with a whole set of characteristics that were just great for taking care of sheep and living outdoors, but were not so good for living in a luxury apartment on the seventeenth floor.

Start with a picture book; get an idea of what dogs you like the look of. Write to the A.K.C. for the addresses of the breed clubs you are interested in, and get some information from them. Talk with people who own examples of the breed. Spend a lot of time with the dogs themselves. Remember that what *you* make of the puppy is more important than what make of puppy it happens to be.

5. WHERE (NOT)
TO GET A DOG

You've thrashed out a lot of questions about dogs. You've decided that its time to have one. You've worked out all the problems about where you live and with whom you live. You've considered breeds and types of dogs, and you will soon (the next chapter) learn how to pick a puppy with lots of good potential. Now, where is this super-puppy going to come from? There are millions of puppies and thousands and thousands of people who want to sell them to you and give them to you. Where do you start?

We suggest you start by thinking about what has already happened to the puppy by the time you meet him. Was the puppy's mother healthy? Did she have enough to eat, and the right kind of care before the puppy was born? Was the puppy born in a warm, clean place? Were the first few days and weeks of life comfortable and secure for the puppy? Did the dog have a chance to get to know some *people* during the first days of life? Has a veterinarian examined the puppy? Was the dog treated for worms? What sort of personality has the puppy inherited from its parents?

You can't be certain about any of these things unless you were right there from the moment the puppy was born, or even earlier. You have to guess, take someone else's word, and leave it to chance that your puppy got the best possible start in life. But you can narrow the chances down quite a bit by being careful about the place where you get your puppy, and the people who are responsible for the dog until the time it goes home with you. The way your puppy was treated during its first days has a lot to do with the way the pup will respond to your care. You want to be as sure as you can be that the pup started out being treated as well as you are going to treat it.

It would be very difficult if not impossible to find a puppy in whose life everything had happened perfectly in the development of his personality and health. What you have to do is look for a puppy with the best record possible. Most people will get their puppy from one of the following: pet shops, breeders, animal shelters and pounds, friends or neighbors. With the exception of pet shops which are always bad, the other sources can be good or bad places to get a new puppy or dog. Let's examine them one at a time.

PET SHOPS: A pet shop is a good place to buy a leash and collar, or dog vitamins, but it is the worst place to buy a puppy. For our purposes there are no exceptions; there may be a few good pet shops that sell dogs and cats, but your chances of finding one are very slim. There are many modern pet shops with carpeting and indirect lighting, and piped-in music. The salesmen have nifty uniforms or white coats like dentists. These pet shops are no good. There are friendly little neighborhood pet shops, with a kindly old man behind the counter, who is nice to everyone and loves to give advice about animals. These pet shops are no good either.

The only good pet shop is one which does not sell live dogs and cats. Here are some reasons why.

1. There are very few laws regulating pet shops. Some communities have local health laws, but they usually address themselves to the cleanliness of the store. These laws do not guarantee that the animal you buy will be a sound and healthy animal.

Pet shops have a very poor record when it comes to the health of the animals they sell. There is nothing sadder than to bring home a new puppy and find out it is sick, even dying. The store may be willing to replace the puppy, but you will have had a horrible experience that you can very well do without. All kinds of puppies and other animals from all kinds of places come to the pet shop; if a sick animal comes in with something catching, it can spread to all the other animals. Puppies arrive constantly; you can't keep a store without something to sell.

Stores have to make money—that's what they're for. They can't spend all of their time, and a lot of money making sure the animals are healthy. There are customers to wait on, records to keep. The man in the shoe store doesn't open every box to see that every pair of shoes is made properly. If something is wrong with them, the customer will bring them back. It is similar in a pet shop. The difference is that instead of sending poor merchandise back to a factory, the pet shop owner sometimes tries to resell the sickly pup, or simply destroys it. It is less expensive to destroy a sick puppy than to have it treated by a veterinarian.

Beware! Most pet shops rely on a sad-looking puppy selling itself to a soft-hearted person. It is difficult to pass by a soft bundle of fur crouched in the corner of a tiny cage. The next time you see such a puppy you might say, "I know the book says I shouldn't buy a pet shop puppy, but this one looks so sad." Buy it and you'll be sad too.

2. Dogs in pet shops are kept in small cages. Cages are no place for a dog to spend days, weeks, or even months. During this time a pet shop dog gets no exercise; this causes weakened muscles, and often a lung congestion commonly called "Kennel Cough." Too often the dog walks or lies in or over its own excrement (and often the excrement of other puppies) and is forced to walk or lie on wire which is neither comfortable nor good for its feet. Crowded cages stacked on top of each other, or lined up in a row, allow disease and worms to spread from one dog to another.

Being caged at critical periods in a puppy's life has been shown to greatly reduce resistance to physical and emotional catastrophe. Elsewhere in this book we recommend the use of a portable kennel (a form of cage) in housebreaking and early training of the puppy. We *do not* believe it is fair or humane to keep a puppy in a small cage for more than a few hours (his sleeping time) at a stretch.

3. You can rarely find out exactly how a dog was cared for before its arrival at the shop. Did the puppy get affection? Was the mother

well cared for? Did the puppy really get the proper shots and nutrition? Was it wormed at an early age? Was the puppy removed from his mother too soon?

If your dog had puppies, would you sell them to a place where they would be kept in a cage until they were sold or got too big and then maybe sent to a pound or destroyed? Of course not. Then what kind of person would sell puppies to a pet shop and what kind of care would such a person give to the puppies before they were sold?

4. Pet shops are apt to overcharge about 300 percent. The dogs offered for sale by the pet shop for $295 usually cost the shop less than $100. A good breeder will sell you a similar dog (probably in much better health) for about $100.

5. Pet shops often misrepresent registration. A purebred dog should come with a numbered certificate, signed by the breeder for you to fill in and send to the American Kennel Club. Mixed breed dogs do not have such papers. Pieces of paper marked "Pet-Degree" or "Pet-a-Gree" are meaningless. Beware of pet shops or puppy farms which advertise dogs such as "Peke-a-Poo's," "Lassie Farm Collies," "Cock-a-Poo's," and "Dutch Huskies." These are not recognized breeds, and the papers which come with such dogs are meaningless. There is nothing wrong with a mixed breed dog, or a dog without A.K.C. registration papers, but don't pay $150 for a dog you can get for free at the pound.

WHAT ARE PAPERS ANYWAY? People are always coming to our school with dogs which resemble German Shepherds. "This dog's got PAPERS," they say, and wait for us to fall down in a swoon of admiration. A.K.C. Registration (better known as simply "papers") is equivalent to national citizenship papers or a passport. A passport will identify you as an American. It doesn't prove that you are a good American or a smart American, or a healthy American. It just identifies you as belonging to a particular country. Sick, healthy, beautiful, or funny-looking, a registered German Shepherd is a registered German Shepherd.

More useful than registration papers to a person who knows something about dogs is the family tree or pedigree. You can find out if many of the dog's ancestors have won championships in the show ring. Have any of its ancestors won titles in obedience? The

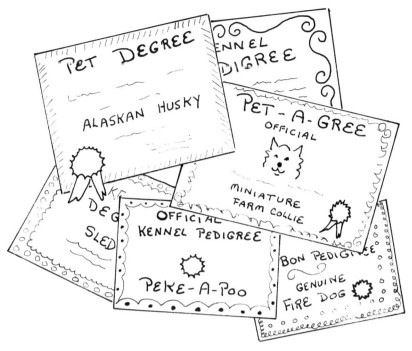

Fake credentials

pedigree will have the letters Ch., for champion before the names of those dogs that have earned it. C.D., for companion dog, C.D.X. (Companion Dog, Excellent), U.D. (Utility Dog), and so on, are obedience titles. Some breeds have special registration numbers in addition to A.K.C. numbers, provided by the breed clubs, to indicate whether a dog has been tested for certain inherited defects common to that breed.

You have to know a good deal about dogs to read a pedigree; otherwise it's just a list of names. You have to know something about the specific dogs and breeders mentioned in the pedigree. The man in the pet shop generally doesn't. What's more, most pet shops don't even have the pedigree on hand for you to see. If they did, you could take a copy to someone who is expert in that particular breed, and ask that person to explain the pedigree to you. The man in the pet shop, if he knows anything, knows that you probably wouldn't buy the dog from him if you could understand the pedigree, or have it explained.

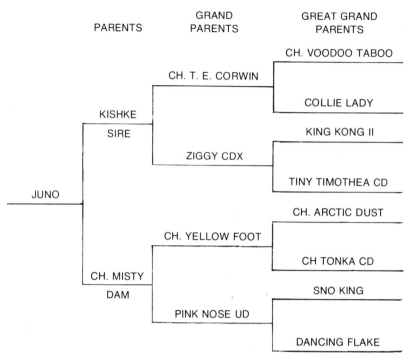

	PARENTS	GRAND PARENTS	GREAT GRAND PARENTS

CH. VOODOO TABOO

CH. T. E. CORWIN

COLLIE LADY

KISHKE
SIRE

KING KONG II

ZIGGY CDX

TINY TIMOTHEA CD

JUNO

CH. ARCTIC DUST

CH. YELLOW FOOT

CH TONKA CD

CH. MISTY
DAM

SNO KING

PINK NOSE UD

DANCING FLAKE

Sample pedigree

An A.K.C. registered dog can be a show quality dog, a pet quality dog with some minor defects (such as a white spot where there shouldn't be a white spot, one crooked tooth, etc.) that you will never notice, or a bad breeding mistake carrying serious genetic faults both physical and temperamental. An ethical breeder will let you know what you are buying, and why you are paying a particular price. A pet shop won't. They'll charge a single price (perhaps $295) for a particular breed, and let you take a chance about quality.

Perhaps the worst thing about pet shops, especially the large chains and department stores, is that they buy from puppy mills.

PUPPY MILLS: The great majority of puppy mills or puppy farms raise dogs as a crop. They are raised like chickens, in cages. There may be a few puppy farms where good care is taken of the puppies, but those puppies can't receive very much care beyond feeding and medical attention. They don't get the human contact they need to become good "people dogs." In most puppy farms, the dogs get little or no medical care. They live in overcrowded conditions, and are forced to walk around and sleep in their own filth. When puppies are shipped from puppy mills, they are stuffed into crates with a lot of other puppies and not enough water. Sometimes the puppies are stuck in these crates for many hours, or even days. Sometimes they are shipped in hot or freezing baggage compartments of airplanes. Many puppy mill puppies die on the way to pet shops, but enough make the trip alive to keep the puppy farmers in business. After all, if you spend little on food, and nothing on medical care, vitamins, or sanitation, raising dogs becomes an inexpensive business to run.

Most puppy mill owners do not try to match the best animals for breeding. Inherited defects such as poor eyesight, defective hips, dwarfism, extreme shyness, and viciousness are common in puppy mill dogs.

If you ever visit a puppy mill and see the pathetic condition of the adult dogs, see and smell the filth, and witness the uncaring way the puppies are raised,' you may want to make a contribution to an organization that wants to close down puppy mills. Three such or-

An overcrowded crate

ganizations are The Humane Society of the United States, The American Dog Owners Association, and Friends of Animals. Until puppy mills are against the law, you have to look out for yourself.

It boils down to this: Under the best of circumstances, you can't be absolutely sure what life was like for your puppy before you came along. In the case of pet shops and puppy mills, it is best to assume that the puppy's early life was horrible, and a poor preparation for living with people. Your best bet is to avoid doing business with any concern that you suspect might fit into one of these categories. What's more, if nobody bought puppies from pet shops and puppy mills, they would have to quit breeding and selling puppies, and go into something more innocent, like selling used cars.

PRIVATE BREEDERS: Technically, puppy farmers are private breeders; on the other hand, a lot of really wonderful people are private breeders. Most breeders fall somewhere in between. You have to decide for yourself what sort of person you are dealing with.

There is some help available to you. Every breed of dog recognized by the A.K.C. is sponsored by a national club devoted to that breed. By now you should have some idea of what breed or breeds you are interested in; the A.K.C. will send you the address of the breed club of your choice.

Let's say you think you might be interested in having a Standard Schnauzer; you write to the Schnauzer Club, and ask them to send you some general information about the breed, and to recommend some breeders in your area. Most clubs will do this. You will still have to make up your own mind about the breeder, but you will have some advance information. Most breeds also have local clubs. You might be able to attend a local fun match sponsored by the breed club, and meet a few breeders. Since most clubs require that their members do not sell puppies to pet shops, you will at least be sure that anyone they recommend as a breeder is not a puppy farmer.

A good breeder loves dogs. A good breeder will only raise one, or possibly two breeds. Such a breeder will not make huge amounts of money from his or her dogs. In fact, good breeders usually break even, or even lose money breeding dogs. Dog breeding, when done right, is more of a hobby than a business.

Good breeders have veterinarian's bills to pay, because they want to make sure their dogs are healthy, innoculated, and worm free. There are also food bills, vitamins, and for some breeds, grooming fees and expensive test breedings to make sure the dogs are free from inherited defects.

When you visit a good breeder, you will find the dogs living in the breeder's house, or in *clean*, dry runs which have access to indoor shelter. Every dog will look healthy and happy, and, if living in a run, will have plenty of drinking water available. The runs should be free of excrement, or, at the very most, have only one pile of droppings per dog. The stool, if there is any, should be solid, not runny. Loose stool is often a sign of worm infestation.

The dogs should look clean, and should not be constantly scratching. Fleas are more than annoying parasites; they carry tapeworm eggs. The dogs' eyes should sparkle, and their coats should look healthy, not dull and dried out. Some breeds shed heavily in spring and fall and any bitch which has just finished nursing a litter is apt to be out of coat. If you see anything like this, examine all the dogs more carefully. A sign of a puppy mill is bitch after bitch pregnant, nursing, or just finished nursing. Good breeders give their bitches a rest between litters.

Try to meet both parents of your prospective puppy, if possible. What shape are they in? Do you like them? Are they friendly?

Check to see if there are hoses and cleaning equipment near the runs. Use your nose. Does the place stink? A good, clean kennel does not smell bad. Beware of excuses from the breeder about poor conditions. Go away and visit another day. Are conditions the same?

How do the dogs greet the breeder? Are they truly happy to see him, or just glad to finally get some attention? Does the breeder really love the dogs, or is he just putting on an act for your benefit?

Ask to see where the puppies are kept. Cold, damp basements or dark garages without adequate heat or light are poor places to raise puppies. Are the puppy quarters clean? Is there water available for the puppies and their mother at all times?

Handle the pups and adult dogs. Check the inside of their ears to see if they are clean. Look for discharges from eyes, ears, and noses. Check stomachs for rashes. Look for sores in the mouth. Do the puppies' stomachs seem bloated (hard and fat) while the rest of their bodies appear thin? This is often a sign of worms. Does the navel protrude unnaturally? A sign of an umbilical hernia.

A good breeder will not rush you into a sale. In fact, a good breeder is as curious about you as you are about him or her. The good breeder wants to know if you will be a good owner for a puppy. A good breeder will show you the pedigree (family tree) and give you much useful information about the breed. *All* good breeders will give you a written health guarantee—a period of time to take the puppy to a vet before the sale is final. If the breeder says this isn't necessary, and besides he's just as good as a veterinarian, walk right out. He's a fool or a crook, and you don't want to buy a puppy from him in either case.

Before making your final decision, play with the available puppies again. Are you really sure that one in particular is for you? (See Chapter 6.) If you are unsure, go away and return another day. If a particular pup gets sold while you are making up your mind, remember that there are millions of dogs available, and only one you.

Pay attention to your first impression of the breeder and the kennel. If you started out feeling uneasy, and wound up being charmed, go away and think it over. Are you reacting to what you saw, or what you were told?

ANIMAL SHELTERS AND POUNDS: A pound or shelter can be a good place to find a dog—if you are careful. If you make the decision to adopt a puppy or dog from such an organization, you will be rescuing an animal in serious need. Read this section carefully before visiting any pound or shelter. It is difficult to windowshop in these places without leaving with an animal.

There are basically four kinds of animal shelters and pounds; the city-run pound, the privately contracted pound that is run for a city or county, shelters run by non-profit organizations, such as humane societies, and shelters run by private individuals, sometimes for profit. In all four categories, there are good and bad places. Sometimes the shelters run for profit are better than those run by organizations such as the ASPCA—sometimes not. The only way to judge quality is by visiting and looking around.

A pound, be it city run or privately run for a city, is a place where dog catchers bring strays, and people dump unwanted animals.

Most pounds have a policy of extermination after a short period of time. A pound's major job is to keep strays off the streets of cities and towns. Extermination becomes necessary, especially in large cities, because there is simply not enough money or space to feed and house the ever-increasing number of stray dogs and cats. A healthy dog or cat taken to a pound usually has between seven and ten days in which to be adopted. At the end of that time, it is destroyed. Some pounds have a policy of selling these unwanted animals to laboratories for experimentation.

The exceptions are usually purebred dogs. Some pounds, such as the ASPCA in New York City, have a waiting list of people wanting to adopt purebreds. Some pounds simply give purebreds an extra few days in which to be adopted.

Pounds destroy animals in two ways. The first is a humane, painless injection which puts the animal to sleep, and finally stops its heart. The second is a method used by larger pounds; it is a decompression chamber big enough to kill a number of animals at once. The air is drawn out of the chamber, and the animals suffocate. The smallest animals, needing less oxygen, die last.

Each year, approximately 33 million puppies and kittens are born in the United States. Since there are only about 8 million homes which take in these animals about 25 million dogs and cats are without any prospect of homes *each year*. Many of these wind up in shelters and pounds; the rest are doomed to live as strays until they starve to death, die of disease, or die in accidents.

If people would neuter their pets, and stop thinking that it is simply adorable to produce litters of unwanted animals, part of the problem would be solved. Until then, people who run pounds and shelters must take the responsibility for these unwanted animals, and solve the problem as best they can. You, of course, help when you adopt one of these animals.

The authors will never forget a nightmarish experience. We were visiting a local shelter to look at a fine Siberian Husky puppy for adoption. A family, mother and father, three children, two cats, and twelve kittens came in. "Yes, both cats had kittens at once—twelve in all," the father said. The family looked happy, they were all smiling. They left the twelve kittens and the two mother cats at the shelter. It was too much trouble to have kittens all the time, and too expensive to have the adult cats spayed. Their children were with them, learning from mother and father that this is the way we treat animals when they get to be troublesome. Just take them to the pound; they will all go to good homes. They will *not!* They will, in all probability, die terrified. You'll know when you're in a bad pound. Unfortunately, the dogs know it too. It stinks. There is an atmosphere of terror. The staff is stupid and probably cruel. Get out. There's nothing here for you.

Both types of shelters, the privately run and the non-profit shelters, take in stray animals. Some shelters never destroy healthy dogs and cats. However, this policy can be overdone. The saddest (and dirtiest) place the authors have ever visited was a shelter that had hundreds and hundreds of cats and dogs piled on top of each other in tiny cages. Some animals had been there for years and most would never be adopted. They were fated to spend the rest of their lives confined without exercise or affection because the humans running the place were too soft hearted to give them a dignified death.

A good shelter destroys very sick animals by injection. A good shelter has a veterinarian on the premises or on call. A good shelter will try to save injured animals, and in some communities have built retirement kennels for old dogs who have no chance of being adopted. Good shelters have large staffs, either because they have a lot of money, or a lot of volunteers. If you want to learn a lot about dogs, get a part-time job (for no pay) at a shelter. Most good shelters also have outside runs where dogs can be exercised. Good shelters will not allow a sick dog or cat to be placed in a home.

Public education is an important function of these shelters. This often includes inexpensive or free programs for spaying and altering animals to prevent more unwanted puppies and kittens from entering the world.

Picking a puppy or dog at a shelter is difficult. Picking one at a community pound is even harder, because you know there is a strong possibility that the dog you don't take home may be destroyed. It is important to think about this before you make your trip to the shelter or pound, because despite the sadness of the place, you must make a good choice. You can only rescue one dog—select the right one, and give it a good home. You can come back for more later.

Many shelters try to find out something about the dogs in their care. They will have a written history telling the dog's age, whether he lived with children, whether he has a history of biting, whether he is housebroken. Avoid problem dogs until you have had more experience. Not long ago we were visiting a shelter with some people who wanted help in making a selection. There was a very nice dog there and the family liked it, but his history indicated that he had bitten a child. From his age and general behavior, we had the feeling that it had only happened once, and hadn't been much of a bite. Then a little girl of about four came along, and the dog cowered in the far corner of his run. It was obvious that the dog had come from a household where the children were not trained (remember small children can be *very* rough on a dog). The dog had finally nipped in self-defense, and was in the shelter before he knew what hit him. Our feeling was that this dog would not be any problem for us to train, and make a good home for. But he was not for us. He was being considered by a family without experience, and with small children. We advised against this dog and wished him luck.

Quite often you will find a pedigreed dog—a Setter, a Collie, a Shepherd—at a shelter or pound. Sometimes there is a higher adoption fee for these dogs. Beware: don't adopt a pedigreed dog just because you think it is a bargain. Make sure it is the right dog for you. The pedigreed dog may have more problems than the mixed breed in the next cage.

You will find all ages of dogs in a pound or shelter, from puppies too young to be away from their mothers to old animals. Be aware of the problems and benefits of every age group. Very young puppies need special care, food, and handling. Like every dog, they also need innoculations and worm checks. A very young pup may have contracted a contagious disease at the pound if it has not yet received its innoculations. On the other hand, you have a better chance of providing the right influences for later life with a young puppy.

Slightly older and middle-aged puppies are full of energy. They sleep less than very young pups, and tend to get into more mischief. Be prepared to make a determined effort to housebreak as soon as possible. The benefits of older puppies include their being more developed in terms of physical appearance, general health, and personality. You can get a better idea of what the pup will turn out to be. An older pup will also need shots and worming.

Adult dogs have the hardest time getting adopted. They have fully formed personalities, and may have been mistreated by humans. Often they are not as cute as puppies. Remember, pups grow up and lose their cuteness too. The advantage of an older dog is that you can see what sort of personality it has developed. It may already be housebroken and it may also have acquired some bad habits. However, with patience, love, and understanding, the adult dog will learn to fit into its new family. Often the dog understands it has been adopted, and will repay you with a lifetime of love and loyalty unequaled by more pampered animals.

All dogs need to be trained (see the chapters on training later on). Many shelters offer public obedience classes as part of their services. If you adopt an adult dog, or an older puppy, take the course.

When it is time to make a choice, there are a few things you should remember. First of all, decide *before* you visit the pound or shelter the approximate age and size of the dog you want. You will be seeing anywhere from five to six to hundreds of dogs waiting to be adopted. If you do not know what you're looking for, it can be confusing and unnerving. Stick to your original decision about size; don't decide that the perfect dog for you and your family would be about the size of a Cocker Spaniel, and leave the shelter with a Saint Bernard. Stick to your decision about the age of the dog. If, for example, you know that no one in your family has the time to nurse, coddle, or housebreak a very young puppy, don't bring one home.

Don't choose a dog who is cowering in the corner of its cage, and refuses to come to you. Don't choose a dog who is frantically pacing, or throwing himself against the walls, and won't respond to you. Extreme behavior can be a sign of illness or personality disorder. If you have doubts about a dog, give it some time. Leave and come back a number of times during your visit—is the dog's behavior consistent?

Despite all your plans, when you enter a pound or shelter, you might find yourself falling in love with a particular dog. If that happens, follow your instinct—within reason. Remember the problems of a Great Dane in a small apartment. On the other hand, if you don't feel a thing for any of the dogs at a pound or shelter, go home. There will be new dogs the next day or week. It is foolish to adopt a dog you can't love. You've got plenty of time, and plenty of dogs. It's true that all the dogs up for adoption deserve homes. But they are not all going to get them. You deserve something too—a good dog. Take your time, and make a good choice (see Chapter 6).

Ask to handle the dog you are interested in. Spend some time with it before you make a decision. If you can, take the dog to a quiet place, away from all the cages and noise. Does the dog really seem to take to you? Do you really want it? Does it seem sick? Check the dog's ears, eyes, belly, and coat. Look for discharge from the eyes, ears and nose, sores on the belly, and bald spots anywhere. Look for sores in the mouth. Is it scratching a great deal? Fleas are easy to get rid of but tapeworm isn't. If there is a veterinarian on duty, have him examine the dog. If there is no vet, get a written statement from the shelter or pound that you have at least twenty-four hours to take the dog to a vet and return it if it is too sick. A good shelter will try to allow only healthy animals to be adopted. Most pounds will let you have any dog—healthy or sick. Some medical problems are easily cured, some are not. If you take the dog, *go to a veterinarian at once!* It might be a good idea to make your visit to the pound or shelter at a time when you know there is a vet on duty at the shelter, or at his own office. If you can, go to the vet directly, without even taking the puppy home; you may avoid some problems.

You will have to pay a fee or a donation when you adopt a dog. Depending upon where you live, and what dog you take, it can cost you anywhere from $5 to $75. Most adoptions cost $10 to $20. The higher prices are reserved for purebred dogs.

Some pounds also require the purchase of a dog license for another few dollars, and some shelters make you sign a statement promising to neuter the dog you adopt. Ask if they have a low-cost neutering plan. If you are under twenty-one, your parents may have to sign.

Many good pounds and shelters will interview you before letting you have an animal. They want to make sure that you will be a good pet owner and, in some cases, make sure that you are taking the right animal for you.

NEIGHBORS AND HOME BREEDERS: Your neighbor's dog has had puppies. You have known the family and the dog for a long time. You really love the dog, and want one of her pups. You know that she has had good nutrition, much love, shots, and vitamins. You watched the pups being born. How can you go wrong?

On the other hand, if your neighbor's dog is not a dog you like, if the mother tends to be nasty or shy, or sickly, don't take a pup.

Chances are it will wind up with some of the qualities you don't especially like in the mother.

If you see an ad in the local paper advertising pups for sale or adoption, treat the whole situation as you would a visit to a breeder or shelter. Don't assume that every puppy born in someone's kitchen or under the front porch is a good puppy for you.

STRAY DOGS: One day you find a lost puppy or dog on your porch, on your lawn, in front of your apartment building, or in the school yard. It's hungry, thirsty, and very friendly. What do you do?

Before you can consider keeping a stray puppy or dog, you must try to find out if it belongs to someone and is simply lost. See if it has a collar with tags, or a tag riveted to the collar, with a name or a telephone number.

Dogs *do* get lost from homes where they are loved. It is not up to you to punish the family whose dog it is, and if the dog is hungry or dirty, it may not be the result of owner neglect but of days of being lost. If your dog ever gets lost, you will have to rely on the help of people who may find him. Make a good try at finding the owners of any stray you come across. Call the owner, if the dog has a proper identification tag. If the dog has a rabies innoculation tag with a veterinarian's name and number, call the vet. Call the local pound and the police and give them a careful description of the dog. Check the classified ads in the newspaper for several days.

You may want to place an ad yourself. The dog can't tell you how long it has been lost and maybe its owner has quit advertising after a couple of weeks.

If you absolutely cannot locate any clue to ownership, and you do not want to keep the dog, don't just turn it loose. Take it to the local humane society, police station, or pound.

Warning. Don't approach any stray that seems mean or afraid of people. If a shy dog finally approaches you, fine. Just don't move at the dog suddenly, or loom over it. Don't run after it and never try to corner it. When cornered, a frightened or sick dog may bite out of fear. Don't approach a dog which seems to be exhibiting strange behavior (look at the description of rabies symptoms in Chapter 8). If you are suspicious, call the local dog warden or the police.

If you and your family decide that the stray on your doorstep would be a suitable dog for you and your family, and you cannot locate the owner, treat the dog exactly as though you had just adopted it from a pound or shelter. Take it to a vet immediately, and watch out for fleas and ticks.

OSCAR: One of the finest dogs we have known was a stray who had been living in an old abandoned car. He was a hound of some kind, or kinds. He bore the scars of many battles, and had buckshot under his skin where he had once been shot. He was adopted by our friend Peter, who trained him, cared for his health, and became his great friend. Oscar was a gentleman; we never knew him to behave inappropriately. He is gone now, but his friends will always remember him—an example of how a stray dog can sometimes become the ideal pet. So if your stray friend is healthy or curable, and you and your family love it, buy a dog license, and accept our wishes for the very best of luck.

6. HOW TO PICK A PUPPY

The puppy farmer was big and fat. He wore long woolen underwear and dirty overalls. He needed a shave. A man and woman were sitting in the living room of the puppy farmer's house; they had come to buy a puppy. The puppy farmer sent his wife to bring back one litter after another from the basement. The prospective buyers didn't see the basement. "There are some new-born pups down there," the puppy farmer said. "We don't want to disturb the mothers."

Soon, there were five or six litters of puppies romping all over the living room, maybe thirty-five puppies, all Alaskan Malamutes, all black and white or grey and white, all cute, all moving around in a great crowd.

"That one over there has real possibilities" the puppy farmer said, making a vague gesture toward a bunch of puppies who were climbing over one another.

"That one?" asked the man who had come to buy, not sure which he was pointing at.

"That's the one," said the puppy farmer. "A champion for sure. On the other hand, the puppy I showed you five minutes ago is an awfully good puppy too."

"Was that the gray one with the pink nose?" the buyer asked.

54

While all this talk was going on, a very slow moving puppy, who kept nodding off to sleep in the middle of walking, had crawled into the lap of the woman who had come to buy, and gone to sleep. His fur was dull, his belly was swollen, his ribs were sticking out, and he was coughing in his sleep. While the man was talking with the puppy farmer, the woman began to stroke the sleeping puppy.

"How much is this one?" she broke in.

"That puppy is $450," the puppy farmer said. "He's a very high-quality show dog."

The man who had come to buy took one look at the sleeping puppy and panicked. He knew that his wife had a strong tendency to help sick animals and this puppy looked sick to him. He didn't know much about dogs, but he knew they were supposed to be able to walk all the way across a medium-sized room without collapsing. Just then, another double-armload of puppies was brought into the room. Among them was a puppy larger than any of the others. She ran all around the room, and knocked down every other puppy, and some of the humans.

"That's the one I want!" the man shouted. ("At least she doesn't seem to be sick," he thought.)

"A fine choice for $350," said the puppy farmer. "Would you like me to throw in that puppy in your wife's lap for an extra $25?"

And that's more or less how we got Juno, our first Alaskan Malamute. Juno turned out to be a good choice—for us. That is, we didn't really mind that she never stopped running around and knocking people over for the first year and a half. She destroyed most of our furniture, and grew up into a big short-tempered animal, who thinks it is her job to run our house and enforce discipline on the other animals. She has an inherited hip disease, snaggle-teeth, and funny pointed feet. We love Juno, with her faults, but somebody else who paid $350 for a dog like Juno might think they had been cheated just a little. At least we didn't take the poor sick puppy; if we had been able to keep him alive, he would probably have grown up with a lot of problems that would have been hard to solve. The fact is, we're the sort of people who enjoy straightening out mixed-up dogs, but that doesn't mean you should. Maybe you'd rather just have fun with a dog.

By now you know a lot more about dogs than we did when we got Juno. You know the difference between a puppy farm and a responsible breeder; and you know better than to buy a dog in a pet shop. You know how to size up a pound or shelter. You've done some research about breeds, and you've narrowed it down to one breed. You know which breeders in your area seem to be the sort of people you'd trust. Your family is in favor of getting a dog. You have a veterinarian all picked out. You know how much money you will spend. You're ready! The breeder has told you that he has a litter almost ready to leave their mother and you think they all look fine. Which one do you pick?

THE IDEAL PUPPY: The ideal puppy is one which is playful, confident, not too aggressive, and not fearful of new things or people. It will be affectionate toward people, especially you, and it will be confident but respectful toward grown dogs. Not all puppies are ideal puppies. Many undesirable personality traits can be overcome with proper training and handling, but you must decide how much you are willing (and able) to cope with, before selecting your pup.

Is your family noisy? Do people laugh and shout? Are there small children running around all the time? Do people in your family have short tempers? Is anyone in your family bossy or fussy, including you? Are you calm, low-key people? In other words, what kind of environment will your puppy be facing when it comes to live with you? Pups adjust in different ways. If you choose a puppy with some personality difficulties, you have to be sure that you and your family will be able to solve the problems and not make them worse. The following information will give you some foundation for making the best possible choice for the pup and for you.

INHERITED TRAITS AND ENVIRONMENT: No puppy is born fully developed. Puppies are not like automobiles coming off the assembly line. Each pup will inherit from its parents (and grandparents) certain genetic traits which will help form its personality, intelligence, physical condition, and appearance. There is little to do about the physical aspect of the dog, except feed it well, groom it regularly, and make sure it has enough exercise and veterinary care. However, if the dog is going to have flop ears when they should be up-standing, or if it is going to develop hip dysplasia, or if it is carrying genes for dwarfism or some other inherited defect, there isn't anything you can do in advance.

On the other hand, the inherited traits which make up the puppy's personality can be greatly influenced by environment. Environment includes everything that has happened to the pup, and will happen to it during its lifetime. This is why it is so important to avoid pet shop and puppy farm puppies which have had to face a number of traumas in their young lives.

Here are some examples of how heredity and environment work in the development of puppy personality. Let's assume that Penny is a genetically timid puppy. She has inherited a personality which has made her the pushed-around puppy in her litter. She is shy with new people, and is frightened by loud noises. If Penny goes to live with a family which gives her gentle care, if she is patiently introduced to new people and situations and reassured each time she shows fear, she will have a good chance of leading a happy, confident life as a beloved pet. Most likely she will always be somewhat timid, but the love and care she receives will overshadow the inherited trait.

On the other hand, what if Penny had been taken from her mother at seven weeks of age, thrown into a crate and shipped 500 miles to a pet shop? What if she was then put into a cage, where she had to sit for weeks while scores of people peered at her. No petting or friendly gestures, just the feeling she could be "gotten at" from all sides. What would happen if Penny were then bought by a person with little patience, who raised her in a tough, demanding manner, expecting perfection every step of the way? Penny would become more shy and fearful. Her whole life would become an attempt to retreat from a harsh, threatening world. She might even become a fear biter—a dog which bites because it feels it is defending itself, even when no defense is necessary.

As another example, take an aggressive puppy named Charlie. He is filled with confidence, and was top puppy in his litter. Charlie goes to live with a person who is a very bossy individual. This person demands that Charlie absolutely obey at all times, and never express his natural dominance. Charlie is not boss any longer. Far from it, he is at the very bottom of the pecking order. He loses confidence. Everything in his makeup tells him that he must have some opportunity to make decisions, but every time he tries, his owner comes down hard on him. Charlie becomes an uncontrollable piddler, he wets whenever he's petted.

What if Charlie were bought by the opposite kind of person, one who does nothing but indulge Charlie? Charlie would remain top dog, and get to run an entire household; maybe he would get to run a neighborhood too, if he were big enough. We have seen "Charlies" weighing five pounds at maturity, as well as one hundred pounds. We have often seen them in dog pounds, awaiting execution after one indiscretion too many with their teeth.

Neither of the two homes described above were right for Charlie. Each made Charlie into an impossible pet. It is possible to raise a Charlie so that he'll fit in, but it can be tricky—a delicate balance of authority and indulgence has to be maintained and Charlie has to be persuaded to cooperate of his own free will. You can spend a lot of time training a "Charlie." We happen to think it is a very interesting activity but you may not. We get many Charlies and Pennys in our school. Most can be rehabilitated with training—training of the families as well as the dogs. It can be complicated and demanding work. We can't honestly recommend picking a difficult puppy if you can avoid it. There is plenty of challenge and fun in training a puppy with ideal qualifications. Especially the first time around, pick an easy-to-train dog, and avoid problems.

GET TO KNOW THE PUPPIES' PARENTS AND THE PUPPIES:
Have you had a chance to get to know the mother before she was busy with her new puppies? Is the father available for you to see? What sort of personality does he have? Find out all you can.

Ideally, the breeder has been willing to let you observe the puppies at different times since their birth. Even when they are brand new, just a few hours old, there will be some differences in personality that you can notice. One puppy is going to be just a little better than the rest at getting to a nipple. The back nipples produce more milk than the front ones and as the puppies find this out, the dominant ones will take possesion of the back nipples. One puppy is going to have just a little more trouble than the others in finding a nipple. One puppy will be a little larger than the rest, one will be a little smaller. One may be more active, noisier. If you have a chance to see the litter just after birth, take note of these things, and try to remember which puppy was which. Visit the litter often, and see how these tendencies develop and change. Very often, things you thought you noticed about the new-born puppies will characterize

their personalities right along. The one who was best at finding a nipple will grow a little faster than the other puppies, and continue to get more food.

As the puppies start taking notice of one another, and playing, you will find certain puppies taking dominant roles, and certain puppies getting pushed around. Keep an eye on all this, and make note of who is who. Maybe you'll want to take a little notebook, and give every puppy a name or description. Drop in to see the litter as often as possible (every day or two would be best) and make notes about how they seem to be developing. As a rule, it is best to select a puppy which is neither the most dominant, nor the most submissive. You may find that you want one puppy one day, and another puppy the next. This is a good thing to keep in mind. You don't have to make a final choice this early. Do some imagining. Assuming that the bully of the litter keeps most of his characteristics as he gets older, do you want a dog who is used to having his own way, and starts a commotion if he doesn't get it? He can be trained, of course, but you are going to have to convince him that you're worth listening to—maybe convince him lots of times. Do you like your friends to be easy-going or tough guys? Think it over. Look at the puppies. Look at the mother and father. Try to imagine the puppy personalities merged with the mature dogs you have gotten to know. If you are lucky enough to make several visits the litter from which your puppy is going to come, you will know which puppy is yours by the time they are six or eight weeks old. Probably the puppy will know it too. Instinct will work for both of you.

Unfortunately, finding a breeder nearby who is willing to let you visit again and again may not be possible. You will probably have to pick your puppy after only a couple of visits to the kennel. We absolutely recommend that you *do not* choose a puppy during your first and only visit. If a breeder tries to pressure you, leave. You are making a decision that will affect the entire life of a dog and perhaps as much as a quarter of your own life. Do not allow yourself to be rushed. Good breeders will help you make an intelligent choice. Some breeders will counsel against certain pups once they get to know you. There are also breeders who simply want to sell the most expensive puppies first, puppies they feel (or claim to feel) will be "show quality." The important thing for you is to get a puppy which will become a happy, welcome member of your family. If you happen to want to show it, fine, but remember, between shows you will be living with this animal. Choose a puppy which will fulfill the most important dog function—companionship and pleasure.

TESTING: If possible, arrange with the breeder to take the pups in which you are interested away from the puppy pen, one at a time, for a short period. You should spend five to ten minutes alone with each puppy. This should be done when the pups are at least four weeks of age. This is a test, not just an opportunity to play with the puppy; be serious and pay attention.

Before you begin testing the pups, make a small chart, or keep a 3 x 5 card for each pup you are going to test. Indicate each pup by description or name on each card or at the top of each column on the chart. Mark your chart or cards as you test each puppy.

During the testing handle the puppies gently. Do not praise or encourage any of the puppies. Try to say and do exactly the same things with each pup you test. You may already have a preference, but the purpose of this testing is to find out some things about the responses of *all* the puppies. You are not required to take the puppy

PUPPY #1 — (Brown ears)

	1	2	3	4	5
A		X			
B		X			
C			X		
D			X		
E			X		

Sample card for puppy test

with the highest score. If you are really and truly in love with the most rambunctious, troublesome puppy of the lot, take him with our blessing. But if you do the testing right, at least you'll know which one is which.

THE FIVE-PART TEST:

A. Carry the puppy to a quiet area. Put it down in the center of the test area. Walk about ten or fifteen feet away. Turn around, kneel, and gently clap your hands. Don't call to the puppy. Does the pup come to you? How?
   1. Comes readily, tail up, jumps and bites at your hands.
   2. Comes readily, tail up, paws at your hands, and licks.
   3. Comes readily, tail down, licks your hands.
   4. Comes hesitantly, tail down, rolls on its back.
   5. Does not come at all.
Score the pup. On the chart or card, mark down the number of the phrase above which most nearly describes the behavior of the puppy.

B. Stand beside the puppy. Walk away from it. Make sure it sees you. Do not call it, but keep an eye on it. Does it follow you? How?
1. Follows readily, tail up, gets underfoot, bites at feet.
2. Follows readily, tail up, gets underfoot without biting.
3. Follows readily, tail down.
4. Follows hesitantly, tail down.
5. Stays where it is, or wanders away in another direction.
Score the puppy.

C. This step should take exactly thirty seconds. Kneel down next to the puppy and *gently* roll it onto its back. Gently place your hand on its chest for thirty seconds, and hold the pup there. How much does the pup resist? In what Way?
1. Struggles fiercely, flails and bites.
2. Struggles fiercely, flails without biting.
3. Struggles, and then relaxes.
4. No struggle, licks hands.
Score the puppy.

D. Keep kneeling next to the puppy. With one hand, gently but firmly stroke the puppy from the top of its head to its tail. Keep doing this for thirty seconds. How does the puppy react to this petting?
1. Jumps, bites and growls.
2. Jumps and paws at hands.
3. Squirms and licks at hands.
4. Rolls over and licks at hands.
5. Goes away and stays away. (Don't chase it. Count thirty seconds.)
Score the puppy.

E. Stand up. Bend over, and with both hands gently hold the pup under its belly (interlace your fingers). Pick the pup up off the floor or ground (*just a few inches*). Hold it there for thirty seconds, and then gently put it down. How does it react?
1. Struggles fiercely, bites and growls.
2. Struggles, growls, does not bite.
3. Struggles, then stops, licks at hands.
4. No struggle, hangs limply, or licks throughout.
Score the puppy.

FIVE PART TEST

1

2 | 3

4 | 5

After each pup has finished the test, comfort it, talk quietly to it, and return it to its litter. Do not worry if any of the pups relieve themselves during the testing; this is normal puppy behavior. Do, however, note if any of the pups urinate on themselves while rolling over during the testing. This is a sign of a very submissive pup. Comfort *every* pup after testing it, and return it to the litter.

SCORING THE TEST: Category #1. Pups which bite, struggle and flail are dominant aggressive pups. If a pup has scored in category #1 on two or more occasions, it is apt to be a tough customer to train and live with. Such a pup is best suited to a calm owner with great patience, who is willing to put in many hours of mostly non-physical training. Families with small children, elderly members, or short tempers may not be happy with such a dominant puppy. An aggressive pup will exhibit a tendency to nip, and boss people. It will pick on the most helpless members of a family first. Rough-housing or wrestling with such a puppy will provoke nips and bites, and rough punishment may make matters worse. Unless you would welcome a *very* demanding job, leave category #1 puppies alone.

Category #2. If a pup scored in category #2 three or more times, it will probably tend to grow up as an outgoing, dominant dog. Such a dog will respond very well to kind, consistant training, but will be hardheaded and stubborn at times. This would be a good dog for a home with energetic adults who have time to spend training, and lots of patience. Teenagers could also handle such a dog if they were willing to spend lots of time with it. It would *not* be a good dog for a home with young children since it might tend to push them around. A category #2 dog is not apt to bite, just throw its weight around. We like this kind of dog, but don't necessarily recommend it as a first dog. If you enjoy a racket and a good argument, they can be a lot of fun, though.

Category #3. This is the stuff of which superpuppies are made. If a pup scores three or more times in category #3, it will be a good dog for almost any home. It will get along fine with young children, will tend to be responsive to training, and inclined to get to like its family without reservation. Human mistakes and failings will most likely be forgiven and forgotten by this pup.

Category #4. Two or more responses in the #4 category indicate a pup which is rather submissive and easily bullied. Such a pup will need lots of praise and very gentle handling to build its confidence. If there are small children in your home who are rather rough and tumble, it would not be a good idea to get such a pup. However, if there are children in the household who are gentle, and have learned how to handle animals, such a pup would do just fine. If the responses in category #4 are mixed with responses in category #5, the pup is probably bordering on genetic shyness, and that calls for very special, quiet, calm treatment. Such a puppy may never feel totally relaxed with groups of people—and may bite if it feels threatened.

Category #5. We advise that you do not accept a puppy which scores more than one category #5 response. If a pup has two or three category #5 responses it will probably have a lot of trouble getting used to people. If these responses are mixed with responses in categories #1 and #2, the pup is likely to attack people when it feels stress, such as any kind of punishment. A pup like this needs very special handling, and will not be able to forget your mistakes easily. It will rarely tolerate rough handling from kinds.

This kind of pup appeals to many people because it is so quiet and retiring. The people sense its need for reassurance and love. Don't take on a dog like this unless you are prepared to go very far indeed in building its confidence. Dogs of this type should never be owned by people who can't or won't work on introducing them to new situations and people; it is essential that the dog not be allowed to become a fear-biter or barker whenever it encounters a human other than its owner.

What if the test results seem to make no sense, for example, if a pup's results are equally divided between categories #1, 2, 3, and 4? Retest the pup. If you get the same results, it may mean that you are dealing with an animal that is apt to be highly unpredictable later on. You may want to retest the entire litter a couple of days later, and compare results. Reread this section to be sure you're doing it right.

Only under ideal conditions will you be able to follow this testing procedure as we have presented it. For one thing, it involves a lot of time. For another, it may be hard to find a breeder who will go along with it. You may need to modify the test, but at least try to test the puppy or puppies that really interest you.

THE PUPPY AND THE LITTER: Also watch the puppies together. Sometimes a pup which is aggressive toward humans is submissive toward other dogs. Sometimes a pup which is submissive with humans is dominant with other dogs. You should have some idea of your puppy's potential attitudes toward other dogs. Make notes on the litter behavior of puppies you're interested in. If a puppy has been bullied by litter mates, but has strong dominant responses in the testing, he may turn out to be a dog fighter, or bully when he matures. This is a problem you will have to handle through training. If you suspect it, it will be easier to deal with before it emerges as a full-blown problem.

OTHER THINGS TO LOOK FOR: Has the litter been handled by humans in a gentle, friendly manner, or has the litter been kept in a garage and rarely visited? No matter what the genetic make-up of a dog, its socialization begins at a young age. If the litter has been relatively ignored by humans, or if you suspect it has gotten rough handling, go elsewhere for your puppy. Are there young children around the kennel? Are they gentle or rough? Some puppies recover from early difficult or frightening experiences—some don't.

If you are looking at puppies between five and eight weeks of age, their socialization with humans is in the process of taking place. Older pups, twelve to fourteen weeks of age, are much further along in their socialization and their attitudes are pretty well set. Dog catchers (and one of the authors) have had the unique experience of picking up a three-month-old puppy which has never been touched by human hands. It is a fat furry ball of hatred and growling. The younger your new pup is, the more influence you will be able to have on its socialization. An older puppy is a good bet *if* it has been raised with human contact, love, and affection.

Be sure to check the puppy's health. A virus, an ear infection, worms, skin trouble, are all signs of negligent care. Look for dull fur, listlessness, runny eyes and ears (sniff the inside of the ears; a bad smell means trouble). Check the chapters on health care and where to buy a puppy before starting out. You should *not* buy a puppy from a breeder without a health guarantee, which states that the breeeder will refund your money if the dog is sick. Go straight to the vet you have picked out for a check-up and innoculations. Most breeders also guarantee the dog for life against genetic faults. Find out what the genetic problem tendencies of your breed are. Be sure the guarantee states that you can have your money back. You probably will not want to return your dog if he develops a slight hip problem at one year of age, but if the dog has to be destroyed because of some provable genetic defect, you may not feel like taking a replacement dog from the same kennel. We hope you will have picked a good breeder, and that you won't have to worry about things like this.

You've picked the right kennel, the puppies are healthy, the breeder has offered you the right guarantees, and you've tested all the pups in the litter. Now you find that, in spite of all your preparation and scientific attitude, you have fallen in love. There is a particular puppy you know you want, tests and good advice notwithstanding. What should you do?

These procedures are meant to be a *guide* to puppy selection. We hope that by informing youself, using caution, and testing, you will be able to identify the puppies which would be absolutely wrong for you. In the end, your feeling must take over; there must be some chemistry between you and the puppy. You are going to be friends and companions for years to come. If you feel something special for a puppy which is a little shy, or somewhat aggressive (within reason), there is no reason not to have it. But remember that it will take some special care, and extra time. Maybe that's exactly what you need.

Once in a blue moon we come across a puppy who seems unlikely to make a good pet for anyone. For example, if the first thing a prospective puppy does is bite you, hard, he may be saying, "Don't pick me." Take the hint.

Don't take on a problem puppy if you aren't *sure* you can handle it. Think it over twice. With good luck, you will want the good, steady puppy in the litter, which will be easy to raise and train. Remember, no puppy is born a superpuppy. Some pups are born with advantages over other puppies; the best of pups can be ruined by the wrong people, and the most impossible pups can be nurtured and trained into something wonderful by the right people. Choose carefully, objectively, *and* with your instincts and heart. Any puppy you love is apt to become a superpuppy.

7. BRINGING YOUR PUPPY HOME

You've finally decided upon the puppy you want and are ready to bring it home. Bringing a young puppy or even an older dog into your home takes some planning. There are a number of preparations you should make before taking this final step; there are things to buy and things to do. Read the following suggestions carefully.

THINGS TO BUY: A certain amount of equipment will be necessary to make your puppy comfortable. Go to a pet supply store, department store, or hardware store, and get two bowls made specifically for dogs. The best kind of bowls are heavy ceramic, stainless steel or plastic bowls with weighted bottoms. One of these bowls will be filled with fresh water at all times. The other will be used for feeding. If the dog you have chosen is or will be large, get large bowls. Don't create extra expense by buying new bowls every few months as the dog grows. The water bowl for any size dog should be large since all dogs need lots of water.

It is a good idea to purchase a few sturdy dog toys. Most dogs love the kind of toys that squeak; but they can be dangerous. Often they are made in such a way that the metal squeakers are easily chewed out of the toy and swallowed. If the squeakers don't stick in the pup's throat, they will probably stick in his intestines. Look squeak toys over carefully before you buy. Juno has always insisted on rubber mice (bright yellow only),* disdaining any other sort of toy. For Juno's protection, we just cut the squeaker out when we buy the toy. Tug toys are a good idea, especially if there are young children in the home. The puppy can play tug of war with a toy instead of clothing or limbs.

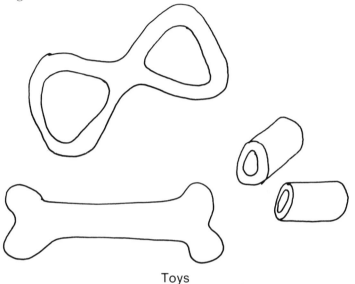

Toys

Go to a butcher or supermarket (if it has a butchering department) and ask for a leg bone of *beef*. Butchers usually throw these away. Ask the butcher to cut off the end joints and cut the bone into three- or four-inch sections. Take these home, trim off any remaining fat, and boil them for fifteen to twenty minutes. Cool them before you give one to the puppy. Keep some of these leg bones in the freezer or refrigerator. THEY ARE THE ONLY KIND OF BONES TO GIVE YOUR DOG—*EVER!* Do *not* let the butcher give you pork, lamb, or veal bones. We don't care how many steak bones your Uncle Herman's Irish Setter ate with nary a problem; a bone can splinter and seriously injure or kill some dogs. The beef leg bone is the only bone your dog cannot splinter. Puppies and grown

* We know dogs are supposed to be color-blind but Juno will *not* play with green, blue, or red mice.

dogs will work for hours getting the cooked marrow out of the bone, and will then use the bone as a teething ring, or for plain amusement. In Chapter 13, we explain how you can make use of these bones to prevent the puppy from destroying property.

If you intend to paper train your puppy, stock up on newspapers (but see Chapter 10 on housebreaking first). You do not necessarily have to buy a dog bed; an old towel, a pair of jeans, or an old shirt will do. If you use old, clean clothing as a bed, remove all zippers and buttons first. Don't be surprised if the puppy refuses to use the bed you've made him and sleeps on the kitchen floor. If you want your dog to sleep on a mat or dog bed when he is mature bed him down in one particular place from the start (see the section on portable kennels in Chapter 10.)

Buy a good leash and a leather collar for the puppy or dog. Don't buy a chain leash since they can hurt your hands, or a junky plastic leash since they have a habit of breaking. Try to find a six-foot-long training leash made of leather or a flat piece of woven webbing. You usually don't find this sort of equipment in a supermarket. Look for a good pet supply store.

If you have a breed that will remain small, you can buy a lightweight leash, about one half-inch wide. If you have decided on a larger breed, the leash should be three fourths or even an inch wide.

If your dog has long hair, buy a rolled (round) collar—it will not grind down the coat. A flat collar is fine for a short-haired dog. In the case of puppies, it is always wise to buy a collar with some room to grow into. If you expect the puppy to do much growing, get an inexpensive collar to start.

A collar should not be tight. You should be able to get two or three fingers under the collar *easily*. Keep an eye on how the collar is fitting—don't forget puppies grow fast. The puppy should wear his leather collar all the time (except when he is being trained). It gives you a handle to grab the puppy by, and a place to hang his dog license, name tag, and rabies tag. Buy a name tag! It is your best insurance against losing the puppy with little chance of getting him back.

Stock up on dog food. The section on diet will explain to you in detail how to feed your pup. Have a sack of dog or puppy food, and a box of biscuits on hand when the puppy comes home.

ORGANIZATION: Before bringing your new puppy or dog into your home you will have to do some organizing. Decide where you want the puppy to live until it is housebroken. A kitchen or family room is a good place. Bathrooms are usually too small, and basements are too isolated and frightening to young pups in most houses. Garages are often damp, and too out of the way. The point is to find a space with a tile or linoleum floor, not too far from the center of activity. If the best place has no door, maybe you can make a temporary one, or a barricade from a piece of plywood.

Take up all rugs, block as many electrical outlets and wires as possible, and remove all plants from the floor and reachable places. You will be able to teach your puppy not to chew on wires and eat houseplants, but it will take a little time. Meanwhile, protect the puppy's life and your property by keeping dangerous and destructible things out of reach.

Plan carefully regarding the day you want to bring the new pup into the home. Pick a day of the week when people will be home to keep it company. Just before a weekend is a very good time. *Don't* bring a new puppy into your home, and then go away and leave it for the day. This may seem like an unnecessary warning, but we have known cases where five-week-old puppies have been left alone in their new homes on the day of their arrival, and have cried and screamed themselves into shock. The first couple of days you spend with the new puppy are critical to your whole relationship; this is the time you are making your very important first impressions on each other.

Plan to bring the puppy into the home when the household will be fairly quiet. Don't plan to have fifteen guests coming on the same weekend the puppy arrives. The new puppy will need adjustment time and quiet before it can face a world of towering humans with confidence.

If there are small children in the house, remove all toys small enough for the puppy to swallow, or chew to bits and then swallow. Your pup can be taught not to chew these things, but not during its first few days at home. If there is a crawling baby, take some precautions and closely supervise the pup and the baby when they are together. This is for their mutual protection, but mostly for the pup's. If the pup is being kept in the kitchen, make sure all cleaning fluids, bleaches, and soaps are out of reach. Don't leave open bags of garbage around to tempt the puppy. If you don't have one, get a can with a lid.

Some house plants are dangerous to animals, especially young animals. Remove from reach all philodendrons, dumb cane (*dieffen-bachia*), and crown of thorns (*euphorbia splendens*). The philodendrons will make a puppy sick, the dumb cane will cause pain, and the crown of thorns is very poisonous.

Poisonous plants:
l. Philodendrons, m. Crown of Thorns, r. Dumb Cane

THE IDEAL WAY: The ideal way to take a puppy home is to spend considerable time with it before it leaves its mother. As it grows, take it away from its mother for short periods of time. Increase the time at intervals, preferably over a period of days. Finally it will be willing to leave with you, and the shock of being away from mother and litter mates will be much reduced. Of course, this is an ideal situation which will not be possible for most people. If you can't arrange it this way, try to follow the other steps in this chapter. If you do, you will be laying a sound foundation for years of pleasure.

TAKE THE PUPPY TO A VET: Before picking up your puppy, make an appointment with the veterinarian you have chosen. Take the puppy from the kennel or shelter directly to the vet. If possible, collect a stool sample from the pup to take with you and ask the vet to analyze it for worms.

Make a note of the shots and treatment the pup is getting on its first visit to the vet, and be sure to make an appointment for a follow-up visit so your puppy can get the rest of its innoculations and another stool analysis. If it is spring or summer, or if you live in a warm part of the country, ask your vet about heartworm medication. There is a special medication for puppies which should be started immediately if there are mosquitos around. If you have adopted an older dog, make sure it gets a blood test for heartworm as well as preventative medication. Pills are easier to administer than liquid; insist upon pills for an older puppy or dog.

The reason we suggest that you take a new dog to the vet before taking it home is twofold. First of all, if it has worms, fleas, or ticks, these can be treated before the pup infests its new home—which is also your home! Second, if there is something seriously wrong, you can return the pup or dog before you get too attached to it. This may sound hard-hearted, but it is not your responsibility to save sick puppies. There are healthy ones being destroyed every day. We would probably sell our house and everything else to pay for medical treatment needed by Juno or Arnold. But they've been with us a while, and we love them. If you see that a puppy is going to have trouble, and you haven't formed a bond with him, give him back! You deserve a healthy puppy.

Before leaving the vet, ask him for some puppy vitamins, and a calcium supplement for the growing pup. These can also be had in some discount drug stores. (Read the labels and compare prices. If you can get something similar for less, don't buy the veterinary kind.)

THE PUPPY COMES HOME: After your visit to the vet, bring your puppy straight home. Don't stop to visit anyone, and don't stop to walk in the park. The pup will be tired and probably will feel a little knocked out as a result of the shots it received. It will also feel lonely for its mother and/or litter mates. Take it to the place where it is going to spend most of its first few weeks. Show the pup where its water is and offer it some food. It might not eat right away. After it drinks or eats, take it outside (or place it on newspapers, if you have decided to paper train it) and reassure it by saying "Good Puppy!" if it relieves itself in the proper place. Decide before the puppy comes home whether you are going to housebreak it right away, and what method is best for you (see Chapter 10).

It is important to remember that a new puppy, especially a very young one, needs a great deal of sleep and a fair amount of quiet. If there are small children in the house, don't let them annoy or maul the pup. Don't let very young children carry a tiny puppy around in their arms. The puppy can fall and be injured and the child will feel terrible. If you have a large family, let a few people at a time get to know the pup. If the puppy looks tired, let it sleep, but don't desert it. Stay around the house; the puppy, or even a new older dog, should not be left totally alone for at least the first forty-eight hours in your home.

On the second day, put the new leash and collar on the pup, and take it out for a short exploration of the neighborhood (see Chapter 12). Let the puppy set the pace. If the pup seems frightened of noises, cars, or people, comfort it. It may seem comical when the puppy dashes between your legs to hide, but its fear is genuine, and should not be laughed off. Talk to the puppy, and encourage it as you are walking. Remember, since the pup doesn't understand English, your tone of voice counts; make yours pleasant and easy to understand, "Gooooood Brutus!" Don't let Brutus pick up any garbage in his mouth—this includes pebbles, rocks and leaves. If he does, remove this trash gently but firmly and say, "No!" in a firm voice, not a shout. The whole world is new to your puppy. During its first walks it will be seeing things it has never seen before. If you want your puppy to develop into a confident dog, you must introduce it to the world in a gentle, gradual manner.

If there are stairs in or near your house, practice walking up and down with the pup. Most pups will have never seen a flight of stairs and it may be frightening to many of them. Begin with a few steps at a time, and coax (don't drag) the pup up and down. Make it a game with lots of praise, "Gooooood Brutus!"

LEAVING THE PUPPY ALONE: We've already cautioned you not to leave your new puppy alone for several days. It would be cruel to

take a pup from its mother and then leave it on its own in an unfamiliar environment. It is doubly important not to desert it if you have disregarded our advice and bought a pet shop puppy, because such a pup has already had its fair share of trauma, and a little more.

On the other hand, you cannot spend every minute of your life with the new puppy. It has to be left alone sometimes and the sooner (within reason) the pup gets used to being alone, the better. Begin by leaving the puppy alone for a few minutes at a time and then returning. It will probably be sleeping alone at night, but if you have left it and returned a number of times, it will begin to get the idea that you will return *every* time you leave it. Over a period of days, leave the puppy and return to it at different intervals, ranging from five minutes to half an hour. In the beginning be out of sight, but not out of hearing distance. Leave the pup with the same words. We always say, "Guard the house," in case there is a burglar hiding in the bushes, waiting for us to leave. It may seem ridiculous to tell an eight-week-old puppy to guard your house, but it will impress your friends when he's grown up, and he will associate those words with the idea that you will return.

PRE-TRAINING THE NEW ARRIVAL: The training of a puppy begins the minute it opens its eyes, or even before, and continues through its whole life. This does not mean that you are going to begin teaching the young pup, formally, the minute it sets foot in your house. It does mean that you have the responsibility and the power to control most of the important experiences in the puppy's future life. If you do this gently, firmly, and consistently, you will raise a gentle friend.

An important part of training is language. Talk to your puppy right from the start. It will not understand the words, but it will soon understand the feeling behind the words. If you belong to a family that doesn't talk much, this is a good time to change that situation. Eventually the puppy will begin to understand certain words, and more important, it will learn to respond to the human voice. Our observation is that people who only talk to their dogs when they want to give a command don't get as good results as people who talk to their dogs as a matter of habit.

Some dogs learn to talk back; they get a very clear idea of what language is all about, and try to use it as we do. Arnold was just in to see me, he wanted to promote a dog biscuit for himself. He lay on the floor some distance from my desk and made an insistant noise at regular intervals:

Arnold: Ooof. Ooof. Ooof. Ooof. Ooof. Ooof.
Me: (*After trying to ignore him*) What do you want, Arnold?
Arnold: (*Gets up and comes closer*) Woowoo! Woowoo!
Me: Out?
Arnold: (*Silence*)
Me: Water?
Arnold: (*Silence*)
Me: Biscuit? (*As if I didn't know*)
Arnold: Woowoo! Woowoo! Woowoo! Woowoo! Woowoo! (*And leads me off to where the biscuits are kept*)

Although I knew what Arnold wanted, I put him through the routine above, as I always do, because I get a kick out of having a conversation with him. In fact, Arnold uses a different intonation and different body language for "out," "water," and "biscuit," his three most common requests.

Dogs use language in communicating with one another. Facial

Play postures

Aggressive   Defensive-aggressive

Submissive postures

expression, voice and "body language" are all used. Dogs also learn to understand human language, and some dogs (like Arnold) learn to "talk." As you get to know your dog, you will learn to recognize some of his signals. Every dog has a style, just as every person has a distinctive voice that friends and family can recognize.

Here are a few signals that your puppy may use to communicate with you.

GIVING THE PAW: The easiest trick to teach a dog is "shake hands." This is because the dog already knows it. He doesn't intend to shake hands in the same way humans do, but many puppies and dogs will extend the forepaw and sort of wave it at you when they have friendly intentions. This is a holdover from the nursing stage when the puppy used his paws to knead the mother's milk sacs when he was feeding. When a puppy or dog makes this gesture to a human, he is saying something like, "I am just a kid—all I want to do is play." A dog may make this gesture to another dog that he feels threatened by.

PLAY POSTURE: The dog's forepaws are on the ground, his rump is high, his tail is waving, he may be barking or growling, but his intentions are entirely friendly. This is an invitation to a game of roughhouse. You will see puppies making this gesture to other puppies all the time.

FEAR POSTURE: Tail down, ears flattened, cringing, eyes averted. Be careful. A frightened dog may be scared enough to bite.

There are many more basic expressions which dogs use to communicate their feelings, and there are some good books (*Understanding Your Dog*, by Dr. Michael Fox is one) which tell about this sort of thing. The best way to understand your dog's facial expressions, voice, and body language is just by observing and living with him. One of the things that makes living with dogs enjoyable is that they are expressive and their expressions are close enough to our own for us to learn to understand them easily.

8. HEALTH CARE

Just like you, your dog may get sick sometimes. Even if the dog isn't sick, it should see a doctor for a regular checkup. Veterinarians are real doctors with much the same kind of medical training as the doctor who takes care of you. They go to school, and earn a degree (DVM). Just because someone takes care of dogs—for example, the man in the pet shop—does not mean that he knows how to treat them medically. Breeders and pet shop people often do give puppies shots and medicine, and there are lots of home remedies for common ailments of dogs. If you want to be sure you're taking proper care of your dog, though, see a vet.

All dogs need regular health care. Don't wait until your dog looks or acts sick to visit a veterinarian. Dogs are sturdy animals, and they often don't exhibit symptoms of illness until they are really sick. Regular checkups, innoculations and stool sample analyses are very important to the dog's health, especially during the first year of its life. A well-cared-for puppy grows into a healthy dog.

FINDING A VETERINARIAN: There are thousands of veterinarians in this country. Most are very good, some are just O.K., and some are indifferent or bad. To find a good vet, begin by talking to people who own dogs and cats. What vet do they use? Have they had an unfortunate experience with a vet? Which one? Was it really the vet's fault? Some people get mad at the vet when their pet dies, even if the animal was old and toothless, blind and arthritic. Animals do get old and die. When you ask people about vets, get a few opinions.

Picking a vet is very much like deciding if a particular breeder is right for you. Our experience has been that vets who treat farm animals as well as family pets are often the best ones. However, there are some ways to judge how any vet will be apt to work out as the person who takes care of your puppy.

First of all, you should be able to get along with the vet. If he checks out 100 percent positive according to the following list, and you simply don't like him, look further. You've got to be able to communicate.

Does the veterinarian. . .

1. Ask questions about the dog's general health, appetite, elimination, etc.?
2. *Always* take the dog's temperature when examining the dog?
3. Handle the dog all over looking for lumps, feeling glands, etc.?
4. Tell you about shots and booster shots necessary for the dog?
5. Tell you about heartworm and its prevention?
6. Ask for a stool sample, to be checked for worms—regularly?
7. Examine the dog's ears, eyes, skin, teeth, and gums?
8. Have an emergency number for evenings and weekends? Is he (or someone) really available for emergencies?
9. Answer your questions? Good vets appreciate questions about health care.
10. Really like to work with animals? (Some vets don't.)
11. Seem to know something about the problems of your breed. For example: Collies and eye problems, German Shepherds and hip problems.
12. Explain to you exactly what he is doing with and for your dog?
13. Explain the nature of the medication he gives your dog?
14. Occasionally admit that he does not know everything?

If you think that the preceding list contains some perfectly simple common sense things that *any* vet would do, please be warned. We have known vets to ignore every one of our fourteen points. If you haven't been able to find satisfactory information about the local vets by talking to your friends and neighbors, use the telephone book. The time to do this is before you have the dog. Call a number of vets and tell them you are considering getting a dog, and you'd like to drop in to see them, just for a minute or two. Have a look at the clinic, and see how the vet impresses you. If you have a friend who is taking his or her animal to the vet, go along and watch the examination. How many of the fourteen points did the vet remember? We have seen a vet examine a dog in two minutes flat, without touching him. How much do you suppose he found out about the animal's health?

Once you find a veterinarian who seems to know what he's doing, and one that you find you can get along with, the best policy is to stick with that vet. Get to know him or her and let the vet get to know you and your dog. Many veterinarians treat old and well-known clients better than new or occasional ones. This shouldn't be, but it often is. Get to be old and well known. Many veterinarians are only as good as you insist they be. Learn to insist; ask questions and expect answers. Remember, your dog can't speak for himself. He depends on you for that.

Don't be embarrassed to ask the vet to spend some time explaining things to you. If you feel that you are making a pest of yourself, then you are doing things exactly right. Until you really know the ropes, know the specific health needs of your new puppy, be a pest. If the vet tries to make you feel like a pest, lose him. He should know that part of his responsibility is to educate his clients in health care.

ANIMAL HOSPITALS: Animal hospitals are usually just veterinarians' offices. Sometimes an animal hospital is run by several vets. Sometimes young veterinarians intern (get experience) under the supervision of experienced vets in these hospitals. If you suspect that the vet examining your dog is an intern and not too sure of himself, ask for the doctor in charge to double check—especially if your dog is sick. Don't be afraid of hurting the intern's feelings. He's there to learn to be a good vet.

CLINICS: There are animal clinics in some locations. Sometimes they are connected with organizations such as the ASPCA, and sometimes they are privately supported. Sometimes they have less expensive rates, but sometimes they are more expensive than regular veterinarians. We know of one big, famous animal clinic that gives the impression that it is a semicharitable organization, but is really a big rip-off, out for profit, and three times as expensive as your local, competent, friendly vet. Do some checking.

One of the problems with clinics, is that you rarely get to see the same doctor twice. Often much of the staff is made up of veterinarian interns, a year or two out of school, who will be moving on soon. You can't establish contact with one vet who will take care of your dog, getting to know it, you, and the problems the dog has had, through the life of the dog. If there is a clinic in your area, and you feel you would like to use it, first find out if it is really cheaper or better than services provided by local vets.

SPAYING AND ALTERING: A number of organizations throughout the country have set up neutering clinics or programs. Often private vets volunteer their services or reduce their rates for these organizations. There are *too many* dogs and cats being born; remember the 25 million excess dogs and cats maturing every year. In 999 cases out of 1,000 there is no reason to breed your pet dog. *Please be a responsible pet owner and have your dog neutered.*

Neutering an animal so that it can't breed does the animal no harm. In the case of female dogs and cats it often prevents problems which tend to develop in the reproductive organs in later life. Neutering *does not* make a dog fat—over feeding and lack of exercise do that. Dogs *do not* miss the opportunity to father or mother litters of pups. Having puppies *does not* help to mature a female dog, either physically or emotionally. Having puppies *does not* calm a dog down. Reproduction in dogs is a purely biological event which they do not miss. If you or someone in the house thinks it would be educational for the kids in the family to watch a birth, get some gerbils or white mice. *Don't clutter up the world with even more unwanted puppies.* If you think your dog's puppies will have a different fate, have homes with all the people who have admired your dog, and so on, take a trip to a shelter. Just a visit. Someone thought the same thing about most of the puppies waiting to be adopted or die. "Poopsie is such a wonderful dog. We just have to have some of her pups," some people argue. They then breed Poopsie to a local dog with bad genetic faults when she is two years old, try to find good

homes for six of the puppies, and keep one, who turns out to be not at all like Poopsie, and not such a wonderful dog. Readers of this book know that what a dog becomes has a lot more to do with what kind of care and training the puppy gets than whether or not Poopsie was its mother.

Many vets will neuter any female dog, but give you an argument if you ask them to castrate a male. We don't know why this is; maybe it is because most vets are men. Arnold is castrated, and very happy. He is not overweight, not lazy or listless (just the opposite), and he is no sissy. We have not been able to find out one medical reason not to castrate male dogs. It eliminates a chance that your dog will take to wandering, and possibly get lost or hurt in search of female companionship.

As your dog reaches sexual maturity, you will notice some outward signs. You'll know that your female dog has gone into estrus (heat) when you notice a swelling of her external genitals and often (but not always) a bloody discharge. This usually first appears between six and twelve months of age, and it lasts about eighteen days. You may notice a lot of male dogs hanging around at this time. Look out! At approximately the middle of the heat period, your dog will be receptive to mating. Usually spaying (neutering) can take place after the first heat period. Talk to your vet.

It is not as easy to tell when males are sexually mature. Often a pup matures sexually before he starts lifting his leg to urinate. Your vet will help you decide the best time to alter your male puppy.

GENERAL HEALTH: You should get to know your dog so well that you are able to see changes in behavior which may indicate illness. Check your dog over at least once a week while you are petting it. The following are some things you should look for as signs that your dog needs a visit to the vet.

1. Any lump under or on the skin that does not go away in a few days.
2. Any rash or inflammation on the stomach, inside the legs, on the elbows, or around the nipples. Part the hair and check carefully.
3. Runny ears or inflamed or encrusted inner ears. An ear infection can be so painful that it makes the sweetest animal nasty.
4. Red eyes, or discharge running from the eyes.
5. Sores in the mouth, or gums, around teeth, on the tongue.
6. Spots of baldness on the face or body.
7. Crusty sores on the body.
8. Sudden loss of appetite.
9. Extreme lethargy (unwillingness to move around and play).
10. Persistent loose bowels or diarrhea.
11. Blood in the stool or urine.
12. Persistent coughing and/or sneezing.
13. Sudden inability to control urine or sudden need to urinate many times a day.
14. Pain when urinating or moving bowels.
15. Pain when petted on sides, belly, or hindquarters.
16. Persistent vomiting after or between meals.
17. Convulsions or fainting spells.
18. Unwillingness to drink water.
19. Physical injuries, deep cuts, injured legs or tail.

In all cases, don't take a chance. Call or visit your veterinarian. Some conditions do clear up by themselves, but many simply get worse and worse. A nice thing about dogs is that they are basically hardy and tend to heal quickly with the right treatment.

INOCULATIONS AND WORMING: All dogs need regular inoculations, worm checks, and wormings. The following information includes a description of parasites, internal and external, and contagious diseases dogs may contract. This is not pleasant reading, but have a look at it just the same. Prevention is easier than curing.

VACCINATIONS—IMMUNITY TO DISEASE: there are two kinds of vaccines given to dogs, the so-called temporary shots and permanent shots.

TEMPORARY SHOTS: This kind of vaccine is antiserum (a cure), gamma globulin, or antibodies received by a puppy when it nurses from its immune mother. It is a *very short-lived* kind of immunity. It only lasts from ten to fourteen days, and is usually used only as treatment for adult dogs or as a *temporary* immunity for puppies five to twelve weeks old.

If you buy a very young puppy with "shots" already given, they will be the temporary shots. Take it to the vet at once.

PERMANENT SHOTS: Active Vaccine. This type of vaccine is made from living or dead disease-causing agents. It is similar to the polio or smallpox vaccines for humans. Although this type of vaccine is often called a "permanent shot" it *must* be renewed yearly in the form of a booster shot. The original series of permanent shots must be given to a pup as soon after it is three months old as possible. Don't wait.

Warning: Only healthy pups should be vaccinated with the active vaccines. A good vet will thoroughly check your puppy, ask you questions about its health, and take its temperature before administering shots. If a vet does not do this, don't let him give the shots. A puppy with an infection or fever can become seriously ill, and even die if given a vaccination of active serum before becoming well.

MAJOR DISEASES COMBATTED BY VACCINATIONS:

CANINE HEPATITIS
Cause: Virus
Disease: Attacks the liver, gastrointestinal tract, and sometimes the
    kidney and brain.

Incubation period: About one week.

Who gets its: All dogs, especially puppies.

How it is transmitted: through urine, stools, saliva of infected dogs. It is highly contagious; you can carry it on your shoes and clothing. You cannot contract it yourself. Canine hepatitis is on the increase worldwide, and can be transmitted by a recently cured dog.

Symptoms: The dog will be well one day and very sick the next. It will be listless, very thirsty, dehydrated, have diarrhea and vomit frequently. There will be loss of appetite, a high temperature, tenderness in the abdomen, and heavy rapid breathing. The dog will repeatedly hump its back, or rub its belly on the floor to relieve discomfort.

Treatment: Go to the vet—fast! Make sure he takes a blood sample.

Prevention: The cure is difficult, so make sure your pup gets its permanent shots at twelve weeks of age, and a yearly booster shot throughout its life.

DISTEMPER

Cause: Virus

Disease: Attacks the body tissues through the mucous membranes. It eventually attacks and destroys the brain.

Incubation period: One week.

Who gets it: All dogs, especially puppies.

How it is transmitted: Through the urine, stool, saliva, and nasal discharge of infected dogs. It is highly contagious, although not to humans. It is carried in the air when a sick dog sneezes, and you can carry the virus on your shoes, hands, and clothing.

Symptoms: Running nose, flat dry cough, loss of appetite, diarrhea, foul-smelling stool, eye discharge, general misery, and depression. The dog will also have a temperature two or three degrees above normal, an extreme sensitivity to light, and sometimes fits and convulsions. The symptoms get progressively worse.

Treatment: Cure is very rare. If you suspect the dog has distemper, take him to the vet immediately. Antibiotics in the early stages sometimes save a dog.

Prevention: The puppy should get its temporary shots at weaning, and then every two weeks until it is ten to twelve weeks old (usually a series of three shots). At that time a pup should get its regular (permanent) shots, a booster in six months, and a yearly booster for the rest of its life.

LEPTOSPIROSIS

Cause: Spirochete (a spiral shaped bacteria).

Disease: Attacks kidneys and liver.

Who gets it: All dogs are susceptible.

How it is transmitted: Through urine of infected dogs and rats. A dog can pick it up by simply licking its paws after having stepped in some infected urine. A recently cured animal can still pass on the disease. On rare occasions, humans can get leptospirosis.

Symptoms: Change of color and very bad smell in urine. Vomiting up recently eaten food. Extreme pain in the abdomen. Gums, palate, eyes, and skin may turn yellowish. By the time this happens the kidneys will have been damaged. The dog's temperature will tend to soar and then drop, and it may pass bloody stool and vomit. The gums may bleed and its muscles, especially those in its hind legs, will become stiff and sore.

Cure: This is a difficult disease to diagnose and laboratory tests are necessary. Very early treatment may save the dog, so go to the vet immediately if you suspect it.

Prevention: Permanent vaccination at 12 weeks of age, a booster shot at one year of age, and then a booster shot once a year for the life of the dog.

There is a combined vaccination called DHL (distemper, hepatitus, leptospirosis). The yearly booster will provide this triple protection for your dog.

RABIES

Many states no longer require rabies shots for dogs. Our policy is to make sure our dogs get their rabies shots every two years. It is true that rabies is on the decline among dogs, but in many areas rabid rodents, bats, and so on, may exist. Why take chances? Rabies is a year-round disease that can be carried by any animal, domestic, wild, or pest (rats). Despite the decline, many towns and cities offer free rabies shots as part of their public health programs. Check your area for this service.

Cause: Virus

Disease: Attacks the nervous system, including the brain.

How it is transmitted: Through the bite of a rabid animal or contact of the infected saliva with a cut or open wound. An animal can transmit rabies three or four days before it exhibits symptoms. Rabies can be transmitted to humans.

Symptoms: Dumb Rabies: the jaw hangs limp as if useless, the tongue drools saliva, the dog hardly moves. Furious Rabies: the dog is irritated by everything he sees that moves. He races around, chases his tail, bites anyone and anything. He will be alert, anxious, and his pupils will dilate. In both kinds of rabies, there will be a sharp change in behavior. Young puppies will come for companionship, and then bite. The animal will have difficulty in swallowing, and won't drink (the virus paralyzes nerves and muscles in the throat and jaw). Frothing may occur because the dog is thirsty (but frothing does not always mean rabies).

Cure: There is no cure for rabies in animals. It is 100 percent fatal. It is also fatal to humans if not treated. Report suspected cases to the police or health authorities.

Prevention: A vaccination at five or six months, repeated every two years.

INTERNAL PARASITES (WORMS): Internal parasites or worms are bad for any dog; they are especially bad for a puppy. They absorb the nutrition meant for growing bones, teeth and tissue, and in some cases they actually live by absorbing the blood of the dog, causing anemia. If you keep your puppy or dog worm free, it will have a better chance to live a long healthy life.

The major problem regarding worms is that many people have the idea that they know all about them. There are lots of myths and home remedies for worms, and once you own a dog you'll hear them from just about everybody. Say thank you, and ignore your helpful misinformants.

Here's a chart which lists some of the most common myths:

MYTHS	FACTS
1. All dogs have worms. It's natural.	1. All dogs *do not* have worms. Worms are parasites which live by robbing the dog of needed nutrition.
2. City dogs don't get worms.	2. Any dog can pick up worms—anywhere.
3. Once puppies are wormed, they are worm free for life.	3. Puppies must have a stool sample checked two weeks after their first worming. They should be rechecked every three months until fully grown, and then twice a year for life.
4. Garlic kills worms.	4. Garlic may kill a few adult roundworms. It does nothing to most other worms.
5. If a dog has worms, you can see them in the stool.	5. Only on rare occasions will a recognizable worm be seen in the stool.
6. Worms can't hurt a grown dog.	6. Worms can kill a grown dog if left untreated.
7. Who needs a vet for worming? You can buy the medicine in supermarkets, petshops, and hardware stores.	7. Supermarket worm pills are practically useless. The only way you can find out exactly what kind of worms your dog has is to have a vet examine a stool sample under a microscope. Each type of worm requires a specific type of medication.

KINDS OF WORMS:

ROUNDWORM (Ascarid), Sometimes called "Puppy worm," develops in the intestinal wall. It is slim, white, from one to four inches long, and can infest a puppy before it is born. Part of its life is spent as an egg in the dog's blood. Roundworms take nourishment from the dog and seriously weaken the animal. Several treatments usually about ten days apart are necessary.

FLUKE DISEASE is something you'll probably never have to worry about. It is a parasite carried in raw fish. All you have to do to prevent it is keep raw fish out of your dog's diet, including those he may find on a beach or lake shore.

HOOKWORM is a small worm with things like hooks on its mouth. These hooks attach to a dog's intestinal walls and help the worm absorb nutrition from the dog's blood. Hookworm can cause serious anemia, and lowers the dog's resistance to other ailments. It can be transmitted to a puppy before it is born, and is common in puppies raised in puppy farms and unclean kennels.

COCCIDIA (Intestinal Protozoans) are microscopic parasites which sometimes infest the dog's intestines. They cause a great loss of fluid and dehydrate the dog. Severe dehydration can cause death, especially in young puppies.

TAPEWORMS are long and flat, segmented, whitish-pink worms which attach themselves to the dog's intestinal walls. They take the dog's nourishment before the dog can use it. Tapeworm generally weakens the dog and can sometimes be fatal to a young puppy. Tapeworms are difficult to cure because they push their heads into the intestinal wall. An entire new worm can grow from one head that has not been removed. Medication, enemas, and at least two day-long visits to the vet are required.

WHIPWORM is more serious, but not as persistent as tapeworm. It is a small, round, tapered worm, which settles in the dog's colon and cecus (equivalent to the human appendix). It multiplies rapidly, and can cause a loss of blood, and loss of fluid through diarrhea. If not treated, it can damage the intestine. A bad case calls for an extremely harsh cure that can sometimes cause permanent damage.

SYMPTOMS OF WORMS: These are some of the general symptoms of worm infestation. A dog with worms may exhibit all or some of these symptoms. The best way to make sure that your dog is worm free is to have a stool sample analyzed by your veterinarian.

1. Listlessness and weakness. 2. Persistent diarrhea or thin watery bowel movements with or without blood in them. 3. Bloated stomach, especially in puppies. 4. Dry, coarse, chalky coat. 5. Persistent vomiting, with or without worms in it. 6. Loss of weight and dehydration. 7. Sleepiness and loss of vitality. 8. Increase of appetite without growth or weight gain. 9. Great decrease of appetite and lack of interest in food. 10. Frequent rubbing of body and hindquarters against the floor. 11. Frequent chasing of tail, and biting at base of tail, and anus. 12. Fainting spells after severe bout of coughing or vomiting. 13. Excessive thirst.

HOW WORMS ARE TRANSMITTED: All of the above worms are transmitted through the stool of an infested dog. It only takes one worm egg to begin a worm infestation. Many worm eggs are extremely hardy. They can remain in the soil or a crack in the pavement for months after all traces of dog stool have disappeared. The dog will walk on such a spot, pick up an egg or two on its feet, lick its feet, swallow the egg, and begin the life cycle of the worm in the dog's system. Dogs can also pick up eggs by sniffing the stool of other dogs. Sometimes they get too close.

You can carry worm eggs on your shoes and bring them into the house. Some dogs like to eat the stool of wild animals and/or house cats—another way to pick up worm eggs.

Tapeworm can also be transmitted by fleas. If a dog bites at, and swallows a flea which is carrying a tapeworm egg, it may become infested. If you buy or adopt a puppy or dog with fleas, keep a sharp eye for tiny, pinkish-white tapeworm segments in the stool or around the anus (they will look like grains of rice). Tapeworm can also be transmitted through eating raw meat, especially raw rabbit, and raw fish. Tapeworm is difficult to detect; the segments may not always be present in the stool, so microscopic examination does not always detect it. If the dog is being treated for other types of worms, it may also pass what look like hundreds of pinkish squirmy worms. These are the tapeworm segments. Scoop some up in a plastic container and take them to the vet for diagnosis.

TREATMENT OF WORMS: Take a stool sample to the vet. It should be collected on the day you take it to the vet. Put it in a plastic container or a plastic bag. You do not need very much, a teaspoonful is enough. The vet will analyze the sample to see if the dog has worms, and what kind. For most kinds of worms, the vet will give you pills for the dog. Write down the instructions. Follow his instructions *exactly*. If the dog has been constipated, tell the vet. Vets generally do not worm constipated dogs.

If you wish, you can leave your dog at the vet's for worming, but most worming only takes a few hours after the pills are taken. For the good of your dog, and other dogs, take the dog to a place where you can clean up the stool it passes during worming.

A *good* vet will either ask you to bring another stool sample in about ten days, or give you extra medication to give the dog after about ten days. This is important, because most worms have a life cycle that makes a second worming necessary to get the worms that were eggs in the dog's blood stream when the first worming took place.

Whipworm can be treated with an oral medication in mild cases, but an injection is needed if more severe. The injection sometimes causes unconsciousness and temporary loss of mobility—a weakened dog can die from this treatment. This is why early detection and treatment is such a good idea.

Tapeworm treatment requires several enemas in the course of a day. This is necessary to assure that the tapeworm heads are removed from the intestine. You must leave your dog at the vet's for a day if it has tapeworm.

PREVENTION: There is no absolute way to prevent the worms we have discussed so far, but there are some things you can do to keep them at a minumum. Keep your dog's quarters clean. Scrub and disinfect any area where the dog has moved its bowels. Use a strong disinfectant. Change the dog's water two or three times a day, especially if the dog puts its paws in the water. Keep your dog away from the stool of other dogs. After your dog has been wormed, be sure to disinfect favorite dumping spots, scrub the dog's feet well, keep all feeding dishes clean, and keep your dog free of fleas. Dogs receiving preventative medication for heartworm (see next section) will also receive some protection from other kinds of worms. Since your dog should be getting heartworm preventative during the summer months, and since most other worms are most active in warm weather, it should be possible to keep your dog worm free or nearly so for long periods. Our dogs have not had any kind of worms for three years now.

HEARTWORM (*filariae*): Heartworm has its own special spot in this book because it is not an intestinal parasite, it is a sure killer, and it is the only worm that is preventable. It used to be a problem that was somewhat restricted to certain areas of the South, and has only spread widely in the past few years. Therefore some vets (who don't keep up on their reading) think it is nothing they need to tell their clients about. Heartworm is found throughout North America.

Heartworms grow in the heart of a dog, clog the lungs, ruin the liver and kidneys, and ultimately kill the animal.

Symptoms: By the time symptoms can be seen, it is often too late to save the dog. The dog will have difficulty in breathing, will lose weight, become nervous and irritable, and cough a great deal. It may faint, or have convulsions after hard exercise.

How it is transmitted: Heartworm is transmitted by mosquitoes. When an infested mosquito bites a dog, the heartworm egg enters the bloodstream. It travels through the dog's system and comes to rest in the heart, where it matures. It releases eggs into the bloodstream, which are picked up by other mosquitoes, and transmitted to other dogs. It only takes one bite from the wrong mosquito.

Treatment: A dog with heartworm is a very sick animal. It must be treated by a veterinarian. The dog generally stays there for a number of days. The medication is harsh, and the vet will not administer it until he has made sure that the dog's kidneys and liver are in good condition. The most dangerous part of the treatment comes after the worms have been killed. You must keep the dog quiet for about four weeks, and hope that the worms pass out of the dog's system without clogging blood vessels and causing death.

Prevention: The only good thing about heartworm is that it can be prevented. Take your dog to the vet for a blood test in the early spring (or as soon as you get the dog if you live in a place where

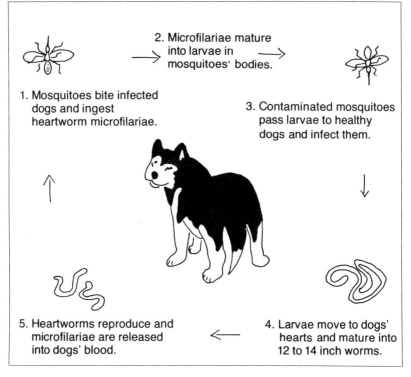

2. Microfilariae mature into larvae in mosquitoes' bodies.

1. Mosquitoes bite infected dogs and ingest heartworm microfilariae.

3. Contaminated mosquitoes pass larvae to healthy dogs and infect them.

5. Heartworms reproduce and microfilariae are released into dogs' blood.

4. Larvae move to dogs' hearts and mature into 12 to 14 inch worms.

Life Cycle of Heartworm

there are mosquitoes year round). It takes about five months from the day of infection for heartworm to be detected in the blood. If the dog does not have heartworm, the vet will give you medication in pill or liquid form to be given to the dog every day, beginning one month before mosquito season, and continuing two months after the season. The daily dose depends on the weight of the dog. There is a special preventative for young puppies. (Hint: we find the pills easier to administer than the liquid. Since many dogs suffer stomach upset when they take the heartworm preventative on an empty stomach, we give the pills just before feeding.)

Anyone who lives in an area where there are mosquitoes and a possibility of heartworm and doesn't protect his dog, is a plain fool, and deserves the misery he's obviously asking for.

EXTERNAL PARASITES (BUGS THAT BITE): There are four kinds of external parasites which might infest your dog: fleas, mites, lice, and ticks. They are more than an annoyance. Most external parasites will eventually cause disease if not removed. They all multiply rapidly, some bite people, and all resist attempts at extermination.

FLEAS are small black parasites which jump from one place on a dog to another, from one animal to another, and occasionally onto a human. They can be found anyplace on a dog's body, but prefer the hairiest places (neck, tail, and chest) depending on how your dog is constructed. The one exception is the sticktight flea which burrows into the skin, lay its eggs, and lives out its life in one place. This flea causes skin ulcers.

Flea eggs go dormant in cold weather, and tend to hatch in the spring. Each flea goes through three stages of life: worm, larva, and adult flea. Fleas can carry tapeworm and can infest the dog's bedding, and eventually a whole house.

MITES are microscopic parasites. Three kinds of mites infest dogs: a cigar-shaped parasite which causes demodetic or follicular mange; a spiderlike parasite which causes sarcoptic mange; and an ear mite which causes otodetic mange. Manges are skin diseases which are contagious and spread rapidly. If you notice scabs, inflammations, bloody pimples, or bald spots on your dog, take it to a vet immediately. If your dog begins to carry its head at a strange angle, or if a smelly discharge is coming from an ear, see your vet. Otodetic mange can cause permanent ear damage.

LICE are stationary parasites which are smaller than a pinhead. Your chances of seeing them are slight. They burrow into the skin and suck and bite and kill hair follicles. A bad infestation will cause anemia. They will crawl onto humans, but dog lice will not stay on a human being, though they will cause irritation.

TICKS are the largest of the external parasites. They have three stages of life, and only one is spent on a dog. During the first and last stages of their life (maturing and breeding), they live in tall grasses, low bushes, crevices around a house, under tables and chairs, in corners, and so on. When they are ready to infest a dog, they will hide in a place where they can drop onto passing animals.

Once on an animal, they burrow their tiny heads into the skin, and hang on; they live by ingesting the blood. They will get larger, and turn dark red when swollen with blood. Ticks are particularly plentiful in woods and in low brush near beaches. A bad infestation can cause anemia. Any tick can cause a local infection, and some carry Rocky Mountain spotted fever.

SYMPTOMS: You will be able to spot ticks and fleas. Examine your dog carefully, especially during the warm months of the year. Check behind ears, near the tail, inside ears, under neck, and in all areas where the legs meet the body (belly side up). Watch for persistent scratching and burrowing into the coat with the paws, tongue and teeth. Watch for bald spots and/or scabby sores.

TREATMENT: Treatments for different parasites differ slightly.

FLEAS: You can use flea powder, spray or soap. If you use the powder or spray, be very careful to protect the dog's eyes. It is best to put the powder or spray on your hand and rub it into the fur (wear rubber gloves or wash *thoroughly* afterwards). Begin by applying the flea killer around the dog's face, ears, and neck. This will prevent the fleas from trying to escape into the dog's nose and ears. Then apply it to the rest of the body. After you do this, spread newspapers, have the dog stand on them, and brush or comb the dog thoroughly. The paper will have a number of dead or stunned fleas on it; wrap them up with the paper and burn, or secure in a plastic garbage bag. If you are using flea soap, begin by bathing the dog's head. In general we feel that flea powder, or a spray in a hand-pump bottle will be easier to control and safer than an aerosol can.

If the flea infestation is serious, take the dog to the vet for a special dipping. With any flea infestation launder all dog bedding with a strong disinfectant, and, if necessary, spray rugs and furniture the dog has used as a sleeping place. Some pet stores sell a special product for this. Spray all corners and vacuum thoroughly.

MITES: Since you won't really notice mites until a dog has developed mange, you must take it to a vet for treatment. He will take a skin scraping and examine it under a microscope. The vet will prescribe medication.

LICE: You will probably have to go to the vet if you suspect lice, because they are so small, it takes a microscope to identify them. He will recommend a dip, powder, or spray—or an oral medication.

TICKS: Ticks can be removed individually, but if your dog has a bad infestation, take it to the vet for a dipping. To remove ticks, soak a piece of cotton in alcohol. Hold the soaked cotton on the tick's body—ticks breathe through their bodies. The tick will back up to try to move to another spot. When you see the head appear, remove the tick. Don't handle it directly—use the cotton, or tweezers, or piece of tissue. Burn the tick or flush it down the drain—*don't squeeze it to death!* Some ticks, in some areas carry Rocky Mountain spotted fever! Never just yank a tick off a dog—if the head stays buried, it may cause an infection.

PREVENTION: TICKS AND FLEAS: New tick and flea collars work. As the collar gets older it has less effect, especially on ticks, which are tough. Flea tags work moderately well. Tick and flea powder or spray work well, especially when applied before the dog goes to the woods, or the beach (if the dog doesn't go swimming). A good brushing after a romp in a likely flea and tick area is a good idea; it removes them before they settle in. Keep your flea powder handy, in case you need it. If you use a flea collar, put it on loosely. If the collar is too tight, it may cause a skin irritation. You should be able to get three fingers under the collar easily. Be careful with flea collars and flea tags if there are small children around—keep the collar in a plastic bag, and slip it on the dog when you go out.

Clean bedding, and a sharp eye for parasites will keep them at a minimum. Lice and mites can be controlled by the methods outlined above—regular brushing, combing, and bathing will help. It isn't hard to keep your dog free of external parasites, if you make prevention routine.

Warning: If your dog sleeps indoors at night, remove its flea collar before bedtime. Place it in a plastic bag near the door and put it on him before he goes out to any grassy areas.

Never leave your dog in a closed car with his flea collar on. The fumes can build up and injure him. Since it is not good to leave any dog in any car during warm weather (even in the shade, temperatures rise well into the 100s in a matter of minutes), this warning can save your dog's health and perhaps life in two ways.

Even with windows partially opened, a dog can suffocate in warm weather.

FIRST AID: There may be times when you have to administer first aid to your dog. Here are some general rules:

1. If a dog has been injured and is in pain, it is wise to tie its mouth closed before moving it. A dog in pain may bite even its most beloved friend.

2. If you suspect broken bones or internal injuries, try not to jostle the dog. It is best to fashion a stretcher out of a jacket or shirt than to carry the dog in your arms.

3. If a dog is bleeding profusely from a leg wound and you think a vein or artery has been severed, apply a tourniquet before moving the dog. Do not do this unless the blood is flowing heavily. Loosen the tourniquet every five minutes and then tighten it again.

4. If the dog has passed out from the heat, pack it in ice, put it in a tub of cold water (hold up its head) or douse it gently with a garden hose.

5. Minor cuts should be cleaned out thoroughly and treated with an antiseptic solution or first-aid cream.

6. If you suspect that your dog has just eaten poison, try to make it throw up by forcing salt water, plain salt (lots of it), a mustard paste

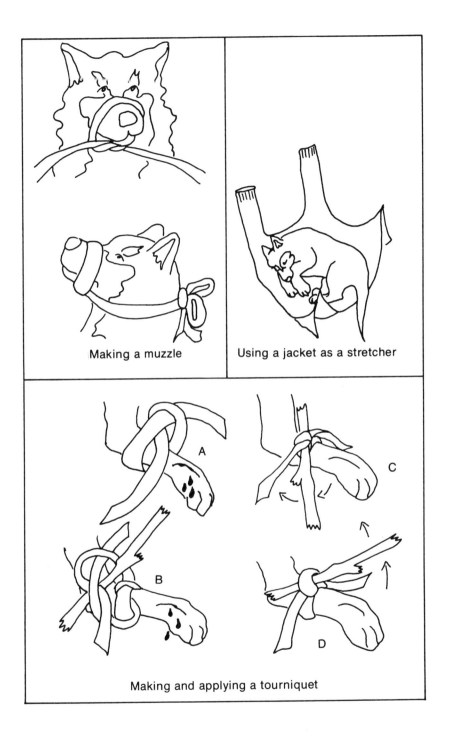

Making a muzzle

Using a jacket as a stretcher

Making and applying a tourniquet

(mustard and water) or a solution of 50 percent peroxide and 50 percent water down its throat. Have someone call the vet while you are doing this. If you think your dog ate the poison sometime before—he'll be vomiting, have bloody stool, general weakness and, perhaps, aimless motion—get him to a vet immediately. Don't make him throw up. If your dog is rigid, *do not administer first aid.* Some poisons, such as rat poison, become more dangerous when usual home treatment is attempted. Get your dog to a vet immediately. *Warning:* Blocks of cooking chocolate and coffee or coffee grounds can be poisonous to a dog. In quantity, these foods can kill a dog.

7. Porcupine quills are very difficult to remove because each quill is barbed like a fish hook. You usually need pliers to remove them. You may also have to have someone hold your dog or you may have to tie it securely to a tree while you remove the quills. If you are anywhere near a vet, get the dog there and let the vet do the job. If you are rather far from a vet, remove as many quills as you can and then go to the vet.

8. Skunking is more annoying then harmful, although if the skunk sprayed the dog's eyes, you will have to bathe them with a lukewarm boric acid solution (or plain cold water if boric acid is not available). Wash the dog in very warm water using tomato juice as a soap. If you really want to deodorize the dog, it will take from two to three hours of bathing and rinsing. Let the dog dry out in the sun or in a warm room. Warmth tends to kill skunk odor.

9. If your dog swallows something which gets stuck in its windpipe, stick your hand down its throat and try to pull it out. If this doesn't work, grab the dog around its body, just under the rib cage. Make your hands into fists and squeeze the dog hard, several times. This forces the air out of the dog's lungs and usually pushes out the obstruction.

10. Drowning is a very rare occurence with dogs but do the following if it occurs: Pull the dog's tongue out of its mouth. If the dog is small enough, hold it upside down and shake it up and down a few times. Then put it on the ground, tongue out. Place both your hands just under its rib cage and push (toward its head) Count to two and then suddenly release the pressure. Do this again. Keep it up until the dog begins to cough and breathe (stop every fifteen seconds or so

Giving artificial respiration

to see if the dog can breathe on its own). Keep the dog quiet and warm for a while. The speed in which you take action counts for all in drowning and in smoke inhalation.

11. If your dog is ever overcome by smoke, give it artificial respiration (as described above) and mouth-to-mouth resuscitation (force your breath into the dog's mouth or nose). If possible, two people should work on the dog at once. The person performing the resuscitation should breathe air into the dog's lungs whenever the person giving the respiration releases the pressure.

12. Fish hooks. Cut off the barbed tip of the fish hook before pulling it out. Clean the wound, apply a first aid solution and watch for infection.

13. Electric Shock. Sometimes a pup will chew through an electric cord. When the pup receives the initial shock, it often urinates. When it urinates, the puppy finds itself standing in a puddle unable to release the cord or move, and it gets electrocuted. However, the pup may not be dead. Turn off the power which feeds the wire or knock the plug out of the wall with a *wooden* broom handle. If the pup is not breathing, give it artificial respiration to revive it. Keep it warm and call a vet.

As a matter of fact, in all cases where there has been serious injury, call a veterinarian immediately. If you know that your vet is on duty, don't hesitate; take the dog to him immediately. In the meantime, get a good book on first aid for dogs and become familiar with its contents (see appendix).

DON'TS WHICH MAY SAVE YOUR DOG'S LIFE:

1. Don't let your dog run near traffic.

2. Don't leave your dog in a car in hot weather. The temperature can build to 150° in a matter of minutes in a car with the windows 'cracked.' This is in normal summer conditions. Buy or make screens for your car or take your dog with you when you leave the car during warm weather. Check dog magazines and pet supply stores for car screens.

3. Don't tie your dog so he can jump over a barrier and hang himself.

4. Don't let your dog hang out of open windows. A passing cat or favored friend has caused many a dog to leap to its death.

5. Don't bandage leg wounds so tightly that the circulation stops. If a bandaged leg begins to swell, immediately undo the bandage.

TEMPERATURE, PILLS, AND LIQUID MEDICINE: Buy a rectal thermometer. Ask your vet to show you how to take the dog's temperature. There is a slight variation in normal temperature depending on the dog's size, but anything over 102° is significant.

Your dog will have to take pills—worming pills, heartworm preventative, and so on. Some dogs will swallow a pill wrapped in a favorite treat, such as a ball of hamburger meat. Most dogs have to be forced to take pills. Put your hand on top of the dog's muzzle, and gently press the upper lips in toward the teeth—the dog will open his mouth. Fold the upper lips over the upper teeth as the mouth opens—this will keep the dog from closing his mouth on your fingers (in order to do so, he has to bite himself). Put the pill as far back on the tongue as you can. Hold the dog's mouth closed, and stroke his throat to encourage him to swallow. The vet will be happy to show you the procedure. Watch out! Lots of dogs are good at spitting out pills when you're sure they've swallowed them.

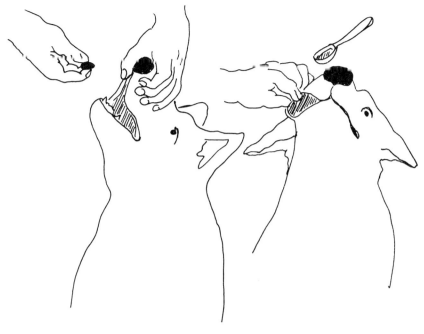

Giving medication

Liquid medicine is more difficult to administer. If you have to give your dog liquid medicine, and you can't sneak it into his food, pull the lower lip near the back teeth out to form a little pocket, tilt the dog's head back, and pour in the dose of medicine. Be prepared to take a shower until you get good at this. If there's a chance to get the same medication in pill form, get it.

HIP DYSPLASIA: Hip dysplasia is common in many of the larger breeds, and also occurs in smaller dogs. Hip dysplasia is an inherited malformation of the hip joint. It cannot be detected until the pup is about six or eight months of age, and then only by X ray interpreted by a vet who understands the disease. It is not always serious; 98 percent of German shepherds have it, and most of them don't suffer very much, perhaps becoming a bit arthritic in old age. Extreme cases can often be helped by surgery. There is an operation which a few vets can perform, in which a new head is built for the femur (thigh bone) out of the dog's own muscle. If you are buying a puppy of a dysplasia-prone breed, find a breeder who knows about the disease, and is breeding with an eye to minimizing it.

ADULT DOGS: Just because your parents took good care of you, got you innoculations and made sure you had medical checkups when you were small, doesn't mean that you can ignore health care now. It's the same with dogs. A dog which was properly cared for through puppyhood will probably be a healthy adult. The dog can stay that way if it has stool samples checked by a vet twice a year, is checked for external parasites, gets his annual booster shots, and receives proper food and exercise. If your dog seems to be sick, call the vet.

OLDER DOGS: Dogs rarely seem to feel age until they are quite old. But, as your dog gets older, it will need special attention. Need to urinate more frequently, more sleep, dulling of vision and hearing, are all signs of advancing age. Some older dogs need special food and vitamins. A dog who has received good health care throughout its life will probably have a comfortable old age.

All dogs have shorter life spans than humans; this is perhaps the worst thing about them. Your dog is almost sure to finish his life before you do. You don't have to think about this all the time, but it is just as well to give it some thought right at the beginning.

It is nice when an old dog quietly moves out of this life in his sleep, after an active and healthy life right up to the end. However, it does not always happen this way. If your dog is so sick and uncomfortable that life is much more pain than pleasure for him, you may have to make the decision to have him put to sleep. Your vet will help you and advise you when you need to consider this—and if it is necessary he can give the dog a painless injection that will put him quietly to sleep. It is painless for the dog, but very painful for the people who will be losing him. It is difficult, but it is part of owning a dog.

IT'S NOT THAT COMPLICATED: After reading this chapter, you may have the feeling that you need to be a licensed vet just to take care of your puppy. The first time we ever looked into a book of dog health care for our brand new puppy, we opened the book to the chapter on canine bloat (a scary ailment—ask your vet about it). We had the feeling that our puppy was sure to die because we didn't know everything about taking care of it. As a matter of fact the puppy didn't die of bloat or any other ailment in childhood. It had its normal share of canine health problems but not all at once, and with the help of our vet, we learned what we had to do to keep our puppy healthy and help her when she did get sick.

With reasonable luck and with some care in selecting a puppy, you will not have much trouble in learning how to take care of your dog's health. Remember, most dogs are hardy animals and tend to stay well; veterinarians are there to give us their help, and whatever health problems your dog may encounter will tend to come one at a time—and you will learn to deal with them one at a time.

9. DIET

Probably more people abuse their dogs through misguided love and ignorance than any other way. This abuse often takes place one or more times a day when the dogs are fed. We have seen proof of the relationship between diet and health time after time. Puppies which have been well nourished will, with the exception of those genetically damaged, grow into healthy dogs. In many cases puppies whose parents are thought to be inferior specimens will grow into very sound dogs when given good nutrition.

It used to take some work and planning to give your puppy or dog good nutrition, but the dog food industry has, in the past few years, made this job the easiest part of dog care. The days of making elaborate diets of meat, cottage cheese, vegetables, and milk are gone—now you can buy good health for your puppy by the bag. There are even special prescription diets for dogs with special problems; people no longer have to spend their evenings boiling and grinding up kidneys for a delicate pet.

Before we discuss how to feed your dog, let us set aside some common myths regarding dog diet.

1. Raw eggs are *not* good for your dog's coat. They do not make it glisten, and they do nothing to improve the dog's skin. In fact, raw

egg white prevents the dog's body from absorbing biotin (an essential B vitamin), and several minerals necessary for good health.

2. It does *not* break a dog's heart if it cannot share the same food the family eats. Table scraps are apt to cause gastric problems, and dogs can easily decide to skip boring dog food (which is good for them), in favor of people food (which, by and large, is not).

3. Dogs do *not* need mostly meat or all-meat diets. It has been a long time since dogs were wild hunting carnivores, and all carnivores derive nutrition from the vegetable contents of the prey's stomach.

4. *No* dog will starve itself to death if it is healthy. Some dogs suffer from temporary loss of appetite. If your dog refuses to eat for more than forty-eight hours, take it to a vet. If it is exhibiting other symptoms too, such as diarrhea and vomiting, go to the vet at once. But if your dog is just holding out for the cheeseburger he saw you eating yesterday, you had better be prepared to hold out longer than he does. "My dog *won't* eat dog food," says the lady with a sick dog whose teeth are rotten from sugar and soft food, and whose stomach is a seething mess from eating nothing but spaghetti and meatballs.

5. Dogs cannot use just *any* bone. Domestic dogs have largely lost the capacity to digest bone particles. The only safe bone we know of is a leg bone of beef, described later in this chapter.

6. Fat puppies are not necessarily healthy. A sleek dog with a thin layer of fat is healthy—but not a butterball or a skinny dog!

7. Candy and sugar do not cause worms. Candy and sugar are bad for dogs or any animal (even humans) because they rot teeth and can cause an imbalance in blood sugar. Food that does sometimes contain worm eggs is raw meat, game, and fish.

DOG FOOD: We said before that dog food companies have made it easy to feed your dog right. They have also made it expensive, for those who think that things are good in proportion to how much they cost. They have also marketed some dog food which resembles people food (and costs as much) to accommodate those people who think that because dog food would not interest them, it must not be interesting to their dog either.

Dog food companies spend enormous amounts of money advertising their products. Each year, some company comes up with a new dog food that looks just like Chateaubriand or Irish stew. Each year there is a new dog food on the market that is "better than all other dog foods." Much of this advertising is just plain bunk, telling the public what it wants to hear. Many of these special fancy dog foods are no better or a little worse than the old standby in the bag; they are produced to satisfy humans rather than dogs. It makes some humans happy to think that little Brutus is eating a canned food that looks and smells like beef stew, or a semi-dry food (loaded with sugar!) that looks like a hamburger. The plain truth is that Brutus would rather eat chocolate brownies or filet mignon if given the chance, but it wouldn't be any better for him than it would for us. The appearance of a food has nothing to do with its nutritional value.

You are not a dog—your dog is not a human. Brutus would be very happy chewing on a moldy old bone. You might not like it. We often meet people in the supermarket who see the 25 pound bag of kibbled dog food in our cart and say, "I wish my dog would eat that." They have some hamburger meat for the dog and an inexpensive can of tuna for themselves. The fact is, our dogs are receiving better nutrition than theirs, and we don't have to eat tuna all the time.

CANNED FOOD: No dog needs an all meat diet, so the 100 percent meat types are not suitable as an only food. You can starve a dog on an all-meat diet. Young dogs can use the calories and fat in canned food but in proportionately small quantities. Grown dogs won't reach their full physical potential on canned food, which is usually about 75 percent water.

KIBBLE: Kibble refers to any dry food which comes in a sack, including meal, chunks, bits, or cubes. You can buy it in two-pound boxes (expensive) or in five, ten, twenty-five, or fifty-pound sacks (cheaper and cheaper). If you keep it in a clean, dry place, preferably sealed up in a metal or plastic container with a cover, it will stay fresh for a long time. It is the lightest, cheapest, best balanced, easiest to store type of dog food you can buy.

There are many brands of kibble available in supermarkets and some companies make a variety of different kibbles in different flavors and styles. We try to stick with brands produced by companies which maintain dog dietary research kennels. Our own dogs have eaten almost nothing but Gaines Meal and Purina Dog Chow for years and years, and they are in fine health, with glossy coats, bright eyes and lots of energy. We switch them from one brand to the other from time to time to keep them from getting too bored with one food. There are other brands which list identical or almost identical ingredients and nutritional content on the bag. Compare and experiment—most of them are pretty good. If you use the Gaines and Purina products as a standard, you can avoid those products which seem to be weak in vitamin and mineral content. This applies to dry dog food in bags. We don't care who makes puppyburgers, and the rest—they cost an awful lot for a comparatively marginal nutrition content. Another note about kibble: Purina Puppy Chow is something we like a whole lot for young puppies.

SEMIDRY FOODS: This includes puppyburgers, fake beef cubes, and whatever the people in the promotion department dream up next year. If you like these dog foods, you probably also bought a Nehru jacket, or sandals with six-inch cork platforms or a car with Zilchmobile painted all across the rear window because someone in an advertising agency told you to; you should have someone responsible carry your money for you. Semidry foods are loaded with sugar and chemical additives. The dog food companies claim they don't do any harm, but we feed our dogs dry kibble anyway.

BISCUITS AND TREATS: Dog biscuits, yummies, and other such products make good snacks for dogs. The large hard biscuits are very good for teething puppies, and will help to keep the dog's teeth and gums healthy when he's an adult. Many dog snacks are enriched with vitamins and minerals; read the box, they may as well add a bit of nutrition to your dog's feeding program. Dog biscuits make much better snacks than cookies, candy, or overspiced table scraps.

BONES: Some dogs can handle any kind of bone, most dogs can't. Don't take a chance with your dog. Give him one kind of bone, and one kind only: *beef leg bones*. They come free from most butchers. It

must be a beef leg—pork, veal, and lamb are too soft or splintery. Ask the butcher to cut off the joints and throw them away, then cut the bone into three to five-inch sections. Take these home, strip off any remaining fat (leave the marrow inside!), and boil the bones for fifteen to twenty minutes. After the bones cool, give one to your dog (or puppy). Keep the rest in the refrigerator or freezer. Boiling the bones makes them harder, prevents decay, and kills bacteria. We haven't met a dog that didn't know what a bone like this was for. They get hours of pleasure sucking at the marrow and gnawing at the bone. Arnold has a favorite that he has kept for two or three years. He occasionally abandons it for a new bone, but always comes back to it. He sleeps with it, plays with it, and tries to take it with him on walks. These beef-leg bones are an important aid in training; they can be used to prevent teething destruction of your property, and they can be used as a sort of pacifier, to help the dog get used to being left alone—and also to get the dog out of your hair sometimes.

SCHEDULED VERSUS DEMAND FEEDING: Some people leave dry food down all day; some people feed the dog at scheduled times. We much prefer feeding the dog on a schedule. That means you have to be home in time to give the dog his meal. It also means that you will know right away if the dog is losing appetite, or is unusually hungry. It also means that the dog's elimination schedule will be as regular as his feeding schedule (very handy in housebreaking), and finally it means that the dog will not get into the habit of dragging bits of food around with him, and leaving little soggy bits of kibble under the couch. If there is any practical way to do it, feed your dog on schedule.

YOUR DOG'S DIET: You should feed your dog according to size, age, and general health. Sickly dogs will need extra vitamin supplements, or even special food; this is to be discussed with your vet. Healthy dogs, regardless of breed, should thrive on the following diet. The only thing to vary will be the amounts—and these will vary between individuals. Just like humans, some dogs burn up calories faster than others. You have to learn by observation how much food your dog needs to keep in shape. The amounts listed on the bag are only suggestions, so experiment.

INFANT PUPPIES: On rare occasions, people have to take care of a puppy too young to be away from its mother—one whose eyes are not even open yet. Perhaps the mother has died, or is unwell; maybe the mother has had such a large litter that she cannot provide adequate milk. If you have to feed an infant puppy, this is how to do it.

First of all, you should provide a warm safe place for the pup. A clean carton with newspaper on the bottom and an old, clean, torn up sheet or shirt (minus the buttons), bundled in a corner of the carton will do the job. A vet can provide a special nursing bottle and some special puppy formula—*do not* feed the pup whole milk. Do not feed the pup condensed milk. If you can't get to a vet, use a commercial baby formula (such as Similac). Mix it with heavy cream and water (one ounce formula, one ounce cream, and six ounces water) and feed it to the pup with the nursing bottle or an eye dropper. The pup will need many small feedings during the day and night (about every three to four hours). Contact a vet for further instructions as soon as you can.

If such a puppy comes into your care, you'll also have to perform some of the other functions of a mother dog. A mother dog licks her puppies on the belly for the first few days of life to stimulate their bowels and urinary tract. If you are caring for a newly born pup, you should massage its abdomen with cotton, or gently rub its anus and genital area until it eliminates; do this about seven to ten minutes after feeding. This massage will also help the puppy to burp. After three or four days, the pup won't need your help in this area. Keep the motherless pup clean (especially after eliminating) with a soft damp cloth or baby oil and cotton.

WEANING: If you own a dog which has had a litter of puppies or if your neighbor's dog has had puppies and you are going to take one, make sure that the pups are weaned properly. This means that each one must have the best possible food in order to make the transition from a nursing animal to an independent feeder. To begin with, the nursing mother should be fed at least three times a day. She should also be recieving special vitamins and a calcium supplement (from the vet) to aid her in producing milk. If she does not receive this special nutrition, she will have a good chance of getting a fatal disease called eclampsia, loss of calcium from bones, teeth, and tissue.

Depending upon the size of the litter, the pups will need extra feedings beginning anywhere from two weeks to three and a half weeks of age. Begin by buying a high-protein instant baby cereal (for human infants, such as Gerber's High Protein Baby Cereal). Mix it with a little lukewarm water, and some canned evaporated milk, canned baby or puppy formula. Remove the mother dog so she does not eat the baby food, and place one or more shallow dishes of this mixture near the puppies. Some puppies need to be taught, some just dive into it. If the pups don't catch on, put some of the food in their mouths. You may have to do this a few times until they get the idea. Never shove a puppy's face into the food dish; the baby glop may clog its nostrils and cause it to choke.

After the puppies have eaten the cereal for about four days, substitute some high protein puppy chow (such as Purina) for one meal. Soak it in warm water until it is mushy before serving. After the puppies have been eating the puppy chow for five days, begin feeding them two meals of puppy chow and two meals of baby cereal per day, plus nursing. The mother will start to allow the pups to nurse for shorter periods of time; she will taper them off as soon as she knows they are getting enough to eat, and are old enough to feed themselves. If you do not begin to wean the pups early, the

mother will nurse them for a longer period of time. This may not be good for her health, or temperament—puppy teeth hurt.

At about five or six weeks of age, the pups should be totally weaned. You will have been giving them four meals a day for at least a week, maybe longer, and the quantities you have been feeding them will have increased as they have grown. Continue to feed the pups four times a day; you may try them out on dry puppy chow. They will enjoy crunching it. They should now be getting one cereal meal and three puppy chow meals a day. Now start buying a good quality canned dog food (such as Alpo), and mix a tablespoon or two with the puppy chow once a day. At the point of weaning, ask the vet for vitamins and calcium supplement powder. Mix it into the feed, or give to each puppy as directed.

WATER: Starting at about three weeks of age, water should be available during meals. If they are making a great mess, splashing and putting their feet in the water, put it in a heavy ceramic bowl. Whenever you see a pup begin to play in the water, tell the pup "No!" in a firm voice, and take him out of the water dish. Even at this age, simple training can begin. As the mother begins to wean the pups, *water must be available at all times,* as it will for the rest of the puppy's life.

SIX TO TWELVE WEEKS: Puppies of this age should be fed four times a day. This is the right age range for you to take your new puppy home. Even if you are not quite sure of a puppy's early nutrition, start feeding him correctly the minute you get him home. He needs puppy vitamins and a calcium supplement from the vet. The calcium is essential for proper development of teeth and bones (and muscle); in breeds which have ears that are supposed to stand up, calcium will help them do it.

The best schedule for a pup of this age is four meals a day:

Breakfast: Baby cereal (high protein) mixed with warm water and puppy chow, vitamins, and calcium supplement.

Lunch: Puppy chow, dry. (If there is no one home to feed the puppy a mid-day meal, make the puppy's breakfast a little larger than the other meals.)

Supper: Puppy chow and a few spoonfuls of canned dog food.

Late snack: (around 9:00 or 10:00 P.M.) Puppy chow, dry.

Water available at all times.

There is no rule for how much any individual puppy will eat. It is estimated that the average pup needs several thousand calories a day in order to grow properly. An adult dog needs less. You have to experiment—some puppies are gluttons, others are light eaters. If your puppy is growing, sleek-looking, no ribs showing, not fat, it is getting the right amount of food. If the pup seems skinny (its ribs showing, and its backbone sticking out), check it for worms and increase the amount of food it is getting. If the pup is beginning to develop a layer of fat on its chest, belly and rib cage, reduce its intake for a while.

Eating styles vary considerably among dogs, just as they do among humans. Some pups gulp their food, and others are delicate eaters. Some pups and dogs always swallow their food whole, others chew every mouthful carefully. This is a function of personality, and may have to do with conditions in the litter early on, such as being the smallest puppy with a lot of big, hungry brothers and sisters.

THREE TO FIVE MONTHS: At about three months, begin feeding your puppy three times a day. You may have noticed that the pup is nibbling at one or more of its meals. This is a sign that it is ready to eat less frequently.

Breakfast: Puppy chow, vitamins, and calcium supplement.
Lunch: Puppy chow, several spoonfuls of canned food.
Supper: Puppy chow
Water at all times.

FIVE TO TEN MONTHS: When your puppy is about five months old, you can begin feeding it twice a day. The size of the portions you feed the pup should be larger than the portions you fed it when it was eating three times a day. The amount of food it eats at this age will be larger than the amount of food it will eat as an adult. Nutrition is all-important for pups in this age range because the puppy will be getting its permanent teeth, its muscles will be developing, and its bones will be growing rapidly. In addition to all this growth, the five to ten month period of puppyhood is a high energy, active period for healthy dogs. Make sure you have your pup rechecked for worms several times during this period; it needs every calorie and every ounce of nutrition to develop properly, and worms rob that vital nutrition.

Be sure to give the pup its vitamins and calcium during this period. Check with your vet on the dosage. Giant breeds such as Great Dane and Saint Bernard need a critical amount of calcium in this fast-growth period. Don't try to figure out your dog's calcium needs yourself. Ask for professional help.

This period of life often worries owners of the larger breeds because of the incredible amount of food the dog will put away. A growing Dane or Mastiff can easily gobble six pounds of kibble plus a can of dog food a day. As we said, the dog's need for food will decrease as it matures, but the larger the dog, the more food you will have to buy. Keep this in mind when considering the breed you will purchase. Shelters are full of Saint Bernards and other large dogs whose appetites outgrew their owners' budgets during the five- to ten-month-old period of the dog's life.

Once again, feed your dog enough so it is sleek looking, and neither too fat nor too thin. Don't ask your neighbor down the street how much he feeds his German Shepherd if you have a Collie or a Malamute. Each breed is individual, and each dog is individual. Arnold and Juno each weigh about 100 pounds and eat about three cups of kibble and a couple of biscuits a day. That's all! A German

Shepherd their size might put away twelve cups of kibble, and not have enough.

Breakfast: Puppy chow, vitamins, and calcium.
Supper: Puppy chow, and some canned food.
Water available at all times. Make sure it is fresh.

TEN MONTHS TO ONE YEAR: Your puppy is now reaching toward physical maturity. We are careful to say "reaching toward" because some breeds of dogs still have months of growing ahead of them at a year of age. The growth during this period will be comparatively slow, but it is taking place. Many breeds continue to fill out and develop muscles for two or three years. You may now switch your dog to one meal a day. Do this slowly. Decide if you want to feed the dog in the morning or evening. If no one is home during the day, we suggest evening feeding. This will allow the dog to relieve itself at night on its last walk, and again in the morning. It is not a good idea to feed a dog in the morning and then leave it alone for eight or nine hours.

Once you decide when the meal will be given, start reducing the size of the meal you plan to eliminate. For example, if the dog is to be fed only at night, make its breakfast smaller and its dinner larger. Keep doing this until you have eliminated the morning meal. You may want to give the dog a couple of biscuits in the morning. (There's no particular reason for this, but it is nice to have breakfast with Arnold and Juno, so we mention it.) It can't be pleasant to be totally empty for twenty-three and three quarter hours a day; schedule a couple of biscuit breaks for your dog in the course of the day.

One meal: ⅔ puppy chow, ⅓ kibble, and some canned food, vitamins, and calcium.
Water at all times.

ADULT DOGS: At about a year of age you should wean your dog onto adult food. Do this gradually—increase the amounts of adult kibble, and phase out the puppy chow. If you switch the diet suddenly, you will probably wind up dealing with a bout of diarrhea. You may stop the calcium pills, and eliminate the canned dog food.

A teaspoonful of cod liver oil is a useful additive to your dog's diet, especially in the winter when steam heat may cause dry skin. Vegetable oil (such as corn oil) will work just as well, but cod liver oil is rich in A and D vitamins, and most dogs love the taste (unlike us). You may also add a little cooked meat fat or drippings to the dry food. These oily additives are good for the coat and digestion, and some dogs need them.

Both of our dogs gobble their food, so we serve it mixed with some water. This prevents them from filling up with dry kibble and then drinking large amounts of water all at once following their meal. This sequence can lead to stomach cramps, and sometimes a condition called bloat which requires *immediate* veterinary attention. Bloat is mainly a problem with giant breeds, so ask your vet about it.

One meal: Kibble mixed with some water, cod liver oil (2 to 4 times a week), vitamins, if your vet advises them, occasional meat scraps, fat, or drippings (once or twice a week at *most*).

Water at all times.

OLDER DOGS: As your dog gets older and less active it will need less food. If you suddenly notice that your dog at age three is getting pudgy, put it on a diet—reduce its food gradually, and watch its weight. Dogs may need different amounts of food at different ages, and even in different seasons. If your dog is getting fat, find out if anyone is overdoing it with table scraps or biscuits. Find out if your dog is promoting snacks from the neighbors. This is common; dogs are good con men.

OLD DOGS: Some old dogs do just fine on the same food they've been eating all their life. Others need special diets. Check with your vet and see if your aging dog needs one.

STOOL EATING: Some pups get into the habit of eating their own stool. This is often a sign of a serious nutritional imbalance, worms, or both. Have a stool sample checked, be sure the pup is getting the correct diet, talk to the vet, and keep the pup's quarters clean. The vet can give you a substance to put into the dog's food. The drug does not taste bad in food, but makes the stool taste unpleasant. This will help break the habit.

Pet shop puppies, and puppies who have had their noses shoved into their stools by ignorant people who thought they were housebreaking the puppy, sometimes get into this unpleasant habit without a dietary lack. Boredom is another cause of stool eating, which fits in with the pet-shop syndrome. Follow the instructions listed above, and give him a lot of attention, and a nice beef leg bone to keep his mind occupied.

FUSSY EATERS: If your dog is a fussy eater, it is your fault. If you have a dog showing fussy tendencies, don't pamper it. You can be on your way to training it to eat nothing but filet mignon. Many dogs will go on hunger strikes in hopes of forcing their owner to feed them canned food, cat food, or steak.

Don't let your dog con you. You wouldn't let a two year old child insist upon and get a diet of nothing but candy. It would be bad for his health. If your dog tries to hold out for something better, remove the food after fifteen minutes, and don't feed him again until the next scheduled mealtime. If it doesn't eat that meal, and you're pretty sure the problem is stubbornness, not sickness, take away the food after fifteen minutes, and let the dog wait until the next mealtime. It isn't apt to go much further—dogs aren't that dumb.

If your dog is a continuous fusser, and you can't go through that many hunger strikes, dress up the food with a half-teaspoon of cod liver oil, a bit of salad dressing, ketchup, whatever he likes. The dog will have won a minor victory, but at least he'll be eating dog food. If you have a cat, add some dripping from the cat food can. (Dogs usually love cat food—which was not designed for the nutritional needs of dogs.)

We have a student at present, a beloved Great Dane, who lives with a large family. The grandmother experimented and found out that the dog prefers eggs over to eggs up. So he has his eggs over. We don't approve, but there is no way to convince grandma; we just hope he gets a mouthful of kibble every now and then.

10. HOUSEBREAKING

The question we are most frequently asked as dog trainers is, "How do I housebreak my dog?" Unfortunately, many of the people asking this question have been living with a dog for six months to a year without doing anything consistent about teaching the dog to relieve himself outside. The telephone call usually goes like this: "We have a German Shepherd, fourteen months old, and he just *won't* learn to go outside." We feel like asking them why they didn't call a dog trainer or read a book twelve months ago. It isn't the dog's fault if nobody gives him a chance to learn the rules of the house.

Dogs are basically clean animals. They sometimes develop habits that we don't like, such as rolling in cow or raccoon dung (they seem to think of it as perfume), but they almost always prefer to keep the home area clean. If you have a puppy who sleeps in his own filth, that's a sign that the puppy has been kept, starting early in its life, in a small cage for too long and hasn't been given any chance to learn to be clean. A normal dog will do its very best not to mess up its sleeping place or the area around it. There is no such thing as a dog who "won't" go outside. What people are really saying when they tell us that is the dog has been allowed to become confused about where it is proper to eliminate. Almost any dog wants to do the right thing, once he finds out what that is. It is your responsibility to help him find out what the right thing to do is.

Young puppies (up to about four months) do not have the physical control to wait very long to be taken out to relieve themselves. How soon the puppy gets control varies from dog to dog. When they are very tiny, they simply dump wherever they are without warning. Soon after that, they will go a little way from their sleeping/playing place and dump there. Very soon, the dog will go a good distance from his home base to relieve himself. Instead of coming down hard on the dog whenever he makes a mistake, (or even worse, coming down hard on the dog *sometimes* when he makes a mistake) and confusing him about where and what is right, take advantage of his natural inclinations, encourage him, and show him the preferred dumping spot (outside).

The most important thing in housebreaking, as in all aspects of training, is PRAISE. Praise works wonders. Our Alaskan Malamutes wouldn't blink if someone hit them over the head with a piano, but if we say, "Gooood dog!" they are all smiles, and wags—and all attention. They spend their lives trying to figure out ways to get us to say, "Gooood dog!" We never say, "good dog," that's like saying, "nice try." We say, "Gooood dog!" with plenty of love and admiration in our voices. If your dog does something to please you, really let him know. People who come to us with older dogs who are still not housebroken have almost always punished the puppy for making mistakes on the floor, without praising him for going in the right place. The puppy gets the idea that dumping or peeing is bad in itself. It becomes a secret messer, dumping in corners or under tables, or it waits until nobody is around and dumps in the middle of the living-room rug.

The next most important thing in housebreaking is time—yours. You or someone in the family must be prepared to take the young puppy outside *many* times a day. You can't overdo this. You are not expected to make yourself uncomfortable every day because there aren't any toilets for you to use. You shouldn't expect a puppy to hold in urine and stool while waiting hours and hours for someone to remember to walk it. After the first few days at home, if your puppy makes a mistake on the floor, it is because *you* didn't give him the chance to go outside. Remember this while you're cleaning up the mess.

We believe that every dog should get at least four walks a day.

Our dogs go out in the early morning, afternoon, mid-evening, and night (as late as possible so they won't wake us up early with an emergency). Many people skip the afternoon walk, and many adult dogs can tolerate this. Puppies can't—they need *more* than four walks, especially young puppies.

METHODS OF HOUSEBREAKING: We will give you a few approaches to housebreaking. Pick the one that suits your needs. Pick one method and stick to it—don't skip around.

THE PORTABLE KENNEL: This is the only housebreaking method that costs money. Pet supply stores sell portable folding kennels. Made out of heavy wire, they are simply cages. You want one big enough for your dog to stand in when grown, but not too big. Remember that dogs don't like to foul their sleeping place. The kennel becomes your puppy's sleeping place. Dogs love caves, places where they can watch what's going on, and still feel secure. If you decide to use this method, it might be a good idea to set up the kennel on the puppy's first day at home. Put a towel or something similar on top of the kennel to make it more cave-like. Introduce the puppy to

A portable
folding
kennel

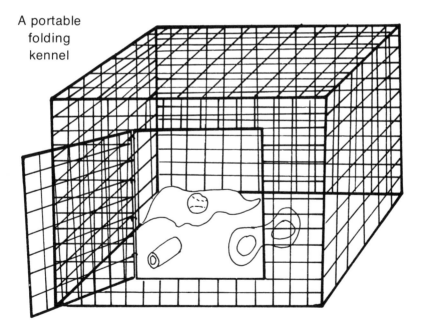

his kennel in a friendly way; give him a treat, put his toys, beef leg bone, and old shirt, etc., inside the kennel. DON'T CLOSE THE DOOR! Let the puppy go in and out. Let him get the idea that the kennel is his own private place. Chances are that he will curl up and go to sleep in it. It is best not to put the kennel in an obscure part of the house. Put it where the cage is out of the way, but the puppy can watch and listen to what's going on. Make it a rule, especially for young children in the family, that when the puppy goes into his kennel, nobody is to bother him. Dogs need privacy too.

Now for the housebreaking part: At night, lock him in. If he's a young puppy, you might want to have the kennel next to your bed so he can listen to you breathe. Make sure he has relieved himself just before bedtime. If the kennel is not too large, he will make every effort not to make a mess in his own private room. In the morning, FIRST THING, take him outside. When he relieves him- self, "Goood dog!" Now you've got night dumping solved, and the rest of housebreaking is simple. We'll give you the details later in this chapter.

Another advantage of the portable kennel is that once you've got the puppy feeling secure in it, you can take his private room with you wherever you go. It is a safe way to travel with a dog in a car, you can take him to motels without giving nervous attacks to the manager, and when Uncle Melvin gets married for the third time, you can take the dog along and set up the kennel in the kitchen. He won't be underfoot, he'll be perfectly content, and you won't have to worry about getting home in time to walk him.

If you use a portable kennel, *don't* use it to punish the dog. Isola- tion is a good punishment but have another place for that. Don't build up unpleasant associations with the kennel.

If the puppy is very young when you begin his night training, he may wake you up asking to be taken outside to relieve himself. It is a nuisance to walk the dog in the middle of the night but do it anyway—and don't forget to praise him when he does his business. A useful trick you can start as soon as you get the kennel is this: Every time the dog goes into the kennel say "go to your room." You can toss a small biscuit into the cage when he goes in on command. Later, when the dog is making a nuisance of himself, you can just say "Go to your room," when he gets there say, "Stay," (he'll learn that later) and there he'll stay, comfortable and secure in his own room. If you have a breed that will get very large, a suitable kennel for night training the puppy may be too big if it is big enough to hold him as an adult. You may have to start small, and get a larger kennel later—save the small one for your next puppy.

PAPER TRAINING: A lot of trainers advise against ever paper training a puppy because the dog is receiving permission to dump inside the house—the very thing you don't ever want him to do once he's grown up a bit. This is good advice. We think you should avoid paper training if your circumstances permit it; we include this section in case it is the only way practicable for you.

When there is a very young puppy, with almost no control, and you live on the fifth floor, or if there will be times when no one is available to take the puppy out eleven times a day, paper training is justified as a temporary measure. Don't be lazy, and let it go too far or you're in for it. We have had year-old dogs brought to us who have *never* moved their bowels outside the house. They will wait for hours to get home to the good old newspaper, or the place where the newspaper used to be, or the rug, which is very like a newspaper if you can't read. And whose fault is this? Paper training is an expedient, it is temporary, it *must* be combined with eliminating outside, or you're asking for trouble.

If you decide that paper training is a good idea for your puppy, begin the first minute he is in your house. Put some newspapers down where you want the puppy to go and show him where it is. Before very long your puppy will start to sniff and circle, or start to squat. Be ready. Pick him up and gently put him down on the papers, "Gooood dog!" Every time he starts to relieve himself, even if you're a little too late, gently put him on the papers, "Gooood dog!" It won't be long before he goes over and eliminates on the papers all by himself. When he does that you should act as though he has just won the Nobel Prize, been elected president of the United States, and struck oil. When he has made it to the paper on his own steam, and been praised for it a couple of times, you can start getting a little tough. Tell him "No!" when he starts to go on the oriental rug, and "Gooood dog!" after you've put him on the paper. He'll catch on.

The big thing to remember when you put those papers down for the first time, is that they will be removed for good—soon. The shorter the time the puppy is relieving himself inside the house, the better it will be for everyone. Don't leave the papers in the same spot for too long. We don't want the puppy to get the idea that it is the spot rather than the papers that makes it O.K. to dump. Gradually move the papers closer and closer to the door the puppy will be using to go outside. This starts him on the way toward going to the door to tell you that he needs to be emptied, and it is also a good location for his messes to remind you that paper training is a temporary thing. If you already have an over-paper-trained dog, try carrying the soiled papers outside and staking them down, or weighting the corners.

Paper training, except maybe for an unwell puppy or the very first couple of days, is *not* a substitute for outdoor housebreaking. The puppy should be taken on plenty of outdoor walks, encouraged to dump outside, and *praised* when he does *during the time that he is also using the papers*. You can also combine paper training with the use of the portable kennel and taking the puppy outside.

Some people (especially with small dogs) never housebreak, and use papers throughout the dog's life. Some people also never take a bath—it depends on how you were brought up. We know of two families who were evicted from their apartments because they couldn't be bothered to empty their dogs outside. The trouble with lifetime paper training, besides being a filthy practice, is that it is never 100 percent effective. A rug has many things in common with a newspaper.

HOUSEBREAKING FOR REAL: Is your dog worm-free? No dog with worms can be housebroken. The first rule of housebreaking is keep your shoes handy at all times. The moment your dog starts to sniff and circle—OUTSIDE fast. Take him near the place he last used to empty himself. "Walk the dog" is a figure of speech, of course; remain more or less stationary, and give him a chance to sniff around and pick his spot. If other dogs have been using the area, so much the better. Stool and urine are calling cards, among other things. Your dog will sniff out who's been by lately, and then he will want to leave word that he's been there too. (There's a dog that Arnold doesn't like who uses a post near our house. As far as I know, Arnold has never seen him. He recognizes him from his

scent, and gives the post a little growl as he lifts his leg.) PRAISE
YOUR DOG. PRAISE YOUR DOG. PRAISE YOUR DOG. It doesn't
matter if the neighbors think you're crazy, you won't have a mess to
clean up at home.

On a piece of paper, mark down the exact time of day when your
dog urinates and defecates. Keep this up for a week. You'll notice
before long that he is pretty regular. Now you know roughly when
he will need to eliminate. All you have to do is make sure you have
him outside a few minutes before things are due to happen. If your
elimination chart does not show regularity, check on a few things.
Is he eating at the same scheduled times? Is anyone giving him a
lot of nonscheduled treats? Is anyone giving him chili, hot sausages,
tacos, lasagna? Does he have a case of worms?

When he makes a mistake, tell him "Bad dog!" and straight outside with him, even though he's in mid-accident, or already empty.
Outside, tell him "Goood dog!" If you find evidence of a mistake,
and you have not seen him do it, go get him, drag him back, and
show it to him, "Bad dog! No!" *DO NOT* shove his nose in it. That's
cruel, and all you will be teaching him is to eat his own stool. After
you've shown him and scolded him, take him outside, "Goood dog!"

Let's go over it again: You know when your dog has to be taken
outside, and he knows that you are going to take him at that time.
You have told him in no uncertain tone of voice that it is Bad to
mess inside the house, and Goood to do it outside. He knows the
rules. He's old enough to hold it in for the few hours between walks.
Maybe you're using a portable kennel, so he simply won't make a
mistake during the night. He doesn't have worms. Nobody is giving
him salami sandwiches on the side. It sounds as though it should
work, doesn't it?

What if it doesn't? First of all, ask yourself if you are giving it a
fair chance. People learn fast and slow, and so do dogs. Maybe he
needs an extra day or two to really get it right. Are you still keeping
a list of when the dog eliminates? Start marking outside elimina-
tions and mistakes. Are there fewer mistakes all the time? Then it is
working. Don't be impatient.

A FEW TRICKS: You know when your dog has to move his bowels
as well as you know anything in the world, and you know he has to
move his bowels right now—only he's stalling, and it's raining, and

you have someplace to go. What now? In your pocket you have a little bottle of Glycerin Suppositories for Infants and Children (and dogs). They look like fat wax kitchen matches, slightly tapered and can be purchased in the drug store. Stand with your legs straddling the puppy (he's facing in the opposite direction), grab him by the tail, lift slightly, and deftly insert one of the suppositories in his rectum. The suppository starts to melt and chances are ninety-nine to one that he'll move his bowels. That's what they're for. "Gooood dog!"

Every time our dogs start to squat, we say, "Hurry up!" While they are eliminating we say, "Hurry up!" When they are finished we say, "Gooood dog!" Now, it is raining, you have someplace to go, the dog is stalling, he's a big dog now, and you don't carry those suppositories around with you any more. You say, "Hurry up!" (you've been saying it to him all his life) and guess what? He hurries up.

If you are having some trouble getting your dog to transfer from papers to going outside (your fault—not enough chances to go outside with praise during the paper training), and he is the one dog in a hundred who can hold onto a suppository, or even two or three, try taking a piece of newspaper outdoors (slightly used is best) and weighing down the corners with stones. If you're in this ridiculous situation, remember whose fault it is.

You've done everything right. The dog is pretty well housebroken, but he is still making mistakes. He's old enough to know better, and you are getting the feeling that he's doing this just to bug you. Also, you are starting to wonder if just saying "No!" is really making an impression on him. Is it alright to punish the dog? Sure it is. Some dogs never need a hard word said to them; others want to test your qualities of leadership. This does not mean you should be in a hurry to whack your dog. Hitting a dog usually doesn't do any good and it certainly doesn't do your relationship any good. The most effective punishment we can think of is isolation. This is how we do it: Fasten a short length of chain with a clip on the end (a chain leash will do) to a (cold) radiator, or some other heavy object. Maybe you can put a ring bolt in the floor in a remote corner of the basement. The chain should be long enough for the dog to sit or stand, but not wander around and explore. Show him what he did wrong. Drag him to the punishment place, tell him "Bad dog!" and attach the chain to his leather collar (not the chain choke collar; you don't want

Isolation

to strangle). Leave the dog (no visitors, no other dogs, kittens, toys) for ten minutes. He won't like it. When you come at the end of ten minutes to release him, he will probably want to apologize. Pretend you're thinking it over for a minute before you accept his apology. Then make friends and forget about it. Don't be a nag. Don't say "Don't you ever do that again!" He was bad; he got punished. Now it is all over and you are both starting fresh.

Please, before you punish your dog, be sure that he is really asking for it. Don't make him suffer for something that is really not his fault. Remember, dogs don't have a time sense like we do. That's why you get the same greeting after five hours that you would get after five days; he can't tell how long you've been gone. Therefore it doesn't do any good to tie him for hours and hours as a punishment. The painfulness of isolation is in the dog's knowing he's done wrong and is being excluded from the life of his family, the thing he cares most about in the world.

If you really feel that you have understood this chapter, and have made a consistent effort to housebreak your dog over a long period of time, and are getting nowhere, call the vet. Make sure the dog is in good health. You may need the help of a professional trainer, but that is very unlikely. Housebreaking is really very easy to teach, and if you are *consistent*, it should work for you quickly. Most of the puppies raised by the authors made one or two mistakes in the house in their whole lives. If you think of housebreaking not as a battle against dirt, but helping a young friend, you should have no trouble at all.

11. GROOMING

All dogs need regular grooming. Grooming includes brushing and combing, bathing, nail clipping, ear cleaning, eye cleaning, and tooth care. Since your dog can do none of these things himself, it is up to you to make time to do them for him. Grooming is more than a periodic beauty treatment—it is essential to good health.

Some breeds need daily brushing and combing. If you are thinking about buying a puppy which will have long silky hair, be prepared to spend a little time each day combing and brushing. Most dogs need to be brushed at least twice a week. All dogs need a human around to clean their ears, clip their nails, and check their teeth. If you are not prepared to do this, you may not really want a dog. There are other pets which require much less care.

AGE TO BEGIN: If you begin grooming your pup when it is very young, you will never have problems grooming it as a mature dog. Get your new puppy accustomed to gentle brushing. Get it used to having its paws handled. Play with its toes, hold them in your hands and gently spread them apart. Talk to the pup—calmly. Play with the pup's ears—gently. Get the pup used to having the inside of its ears touched and looked at. Fondle the pup's face. Look into its mouth, examine its teeth. Gently place your fingers near its eyes, and rub the area around its eyes. Do all of this once a day. When the time comes for you to groom the puppy, to clip its nails, clean its ears, check its eyes and teeth, it will be used to being handled in this area, and will not fight you or be afraid.

THE COAT: Puppy coats are different from adult coats in most breeds. Most puppies have fuzzy, short downy hair which does not look like the coat they will have as adults. Some pups begin growing an adult coat very early, some stay fuzzy until they are about five months old.

An adult dog's coat should gleam with good health. Proper diet, exercise, vet care, and grooming all lead to a healthy coat. If your dog's coat is dull and dry, and if your dog seems to be losing lots of hair all the time, it is time to see the vet. No amount of special pet shop sprays or shampoos will make a sick dog's coat look healthy.

CLIPPING, PLUCKING, AND PROFESSIONAL CARE: Let's do away with a myth. It is *not* a good idea to shave a dog during the summer. A dog's coat is its natural protection against cold, *heat*, insect bites, cuts, and scratches.

There are some breeds of dogs which must occasionally receive professional grooming. If you own, or plan to own, a Poodle or a Terrier (such as a Kerry Blue or Bedlington), you will be looking for a good professional groomer several times a year. You can learn to groom your own dog (many breeders do), but it takes time to learn this skill.

Other breeds, such as Airedales, Schnauzers, Wirehaired Fox Terriers, and Scotties must have their soft undercoats removed at least twice a year, by a method called "plucking." If this is not done, the undercoat grows too long and ruins the curly topcoat. Plucking takes time and patience, and must be done evenly to achieve the proper results. You might want to watch a professional do this several times before you try it yourself.

Some dogs get their facial hair, whiskers and leg hair trimmed. Some dogs need their entire coats trimmed to deepen the color and harden the texture.

Get to know exactly what professional care your dog needs, and what trimming, clipping, and plucking you can learn to do yourself. If you want to show your dog, this is especially important. Breed standards are very strict regarding how some breeds are clipped or plucked.

There are many breeds that do not require any grooming that you can't do yourself at home. All you need is a little time and a few pieces of equipment.

EQUIPMENT: Buy the best possible equipment for grooming your dog; it will then last for years. You will need the proper brush and, perhaps, comb, a good nail clipper or file and the proper shampoo for your dog. You will only need special scissors if you have a breed which must be trimmed and if you decide to trim it yourself. The following sections will recommend specific grooming equipment for specific types of dog coats.

BRUSHING: Each type of dog coat requires special grooming tools, schedules, and methods. Every dog, despite the amount of professional grooming it gets, will need some home care, too. Most of this care comes under the heading of brushing.

Brushing does more than keep dog hair off furniture, clothing, and rugs. It stimulates a dog's skin, helps prevent skin parasites such as mites, fleas, and ticks from infesting a dog, and it keeps many dogs from developing painful and annoying matted hair.

It is a good idea to train small and medium sized dogs to stand quietly on a table or counter top during brushing. This makes it easier for you to reach every part of the dog with a comb or a brush. Large dogs should be taught to stand still on the floor (see Chapter 12). Long-coated dogs should be taught to lie on their sides as well as stand during brushing so that you can work out tangles that tend to form on their stomachs.

NEVER leave a dog unattended on a table. The smartest dog can decide to leap onto the floor, the most agile dog can break a leg.

FREQUENCY: Short coated dogs should be brushed two or three times a week. Medium coated dogs should be brushed at least three times a week, and long coated dogs with silky hair should be combed and brushed daily. The more frequently you brush your dog, the shorter each session will have to be. Most dogs receiving regular brushing only need five to ten minute sessions.

If you ignore the advice regarding your long-coated silky-haired dog and brush it infrequently, it will develop such mats and tangles that it will require veterinary care. The only cure for an extreme case of matted hair is the complete shaving of the dog. This is neither comfortable nor healthy for the animal.

The final benefit of frequent brushing is that dogs which are brushed frequently only need occasional baths.

TYPES OF COATS:

SHORT-COATED DOGS (*Smooth Hair*)
Equipment: medium-soft brush or a "hound glove" (a grooming glove with wire bristles in the palm) and a soft cloth.
Method: Brush firmly but gently with the grain of the hair (in the direction the hair grows). Do not irritate the skin with the wire if you use a glove. The brushing should work out the dead hair and stimulate the skin—like a good massage. Use the soft cloth to wipe away any loose hair left on the surface of the coat.

SHORT-COATED DOGS (*Wirehair*)
Equipment: firm, short bristled brush or a hound glove (see above) and a wide-toothed comb if the dog has straight, fluffy hair on its legs.
Method: Use the same method as for smooth-coated short-haired dogs but, if possible, brush daily. The wire hair tends to trap old dead hairs near the skin. If not attended to, this can create coat and skin problems.

MEDIUM-COATED DOGS (such as Setters, Spaniels, Golden Retrievers)
Equipment: A firm bristle brush and a comb.
Method: Brush with the grain of the hair—gently, but firmly. Be sure to brush the hair from the skin out, not just the top layer of hair. Pay special attention to the 'feathering' (the long hair) on the ears, chest, tail and legs because it tends to tangle and mat. Use the comb to put the coat and feathering in order when you are finished brushing.

LONG-COATED DOGS (*Silky Hair, such as Afghans, Yorkshire Terriers, Lhasa Apsos, etc.*)
Equipment: soft, long-bristle brush and a wide-toothed comb. *Never*

use a wire brush or a fine-toothed comb on a silky-haired dog. They will tear the hair and even tangle it.

Method: Brush and comb daily. Check a picture book to see if your dog's hair should be combed over or away from the eyes. This is more than a beauty treatment. Some dogs with long, silky hair need the hair combed over their eyes for protection from strong light. Others need the hair combed away from their eyes because they are susceptible to eye infections caused by their own hair.

Take one handful of hair at a time and brush it from the skin out. If you don't do this, matted hair will develop near the skin. After you have brushed the dog thoroughly (be particularly diligent around the ears), comb the dog with the wide-toothed comb to make it neat.

LONG COATED DOGS (*Rough Coat*)
Equipment: a wire brush or a stiff bristle brush with long bristles.
Method: Brush at least three times a week. Take one handful of hair at a time and brush, with the grain, from the skin out.

DOUBLE-COATED DOGS (*such as Malamutes, Elkhounds, Pomeranians, rough-coated Collies*)
Equipment: stiff, long-bristle brush or a wire brush.
Method: For dogs with a top coat of medium to long hair and a soft, fuzzy undercoat, you must make sure that the loose hair does not get trapped in the undercoat. They should be brushed at least twice a week—more frequently in the spring when they go into an enormous shed. If you have a female, you will find that she also sheds her undercoat and some of her top coat after she has been in season.

Brush the dog from the skin out with the grain of the hair. Give the area around the neck (the ruff), the hip area, the upper hind legs and the tail special attention. As double-coated dogs shed, their loose undercoat hairs work their way toward the rear of the dog and become trapped. Leather collars tend to trap a certain amount of this loose hair in the ruff.

BATHING: The greatest problem with dog baths is that people tend to go to extremes. Some people never bathe their dogs, and many people bathe them too often. Dogs, especially ones which are brushed frequently, do not need many baths. In fact, too-frequent bathing removes necessary natural protective skin oils. Dogs should not smell too 'doggy.' They should not smell like a perfume bottle either.

A well-groomed dog should be bathed no more than two or three times a year. No amount of bathing is going to remove the odor from a dog which is supposed to smell. If you are bothered by strong odor, do not get one of the several breeds with particularly oily coats—such as certain herding dogs and many hounds. As soon as one of these dogs begins to produce its natural skin oil, its odor will return. Constant bathing will only ruin its coat and skin.

The following are guidelines to follow for bathing. Bathe your dog when:

1. It is dirty. If you find that dirt cannot be brushed out of your dog's coat (let mud harden before you brush) or if the skin of your dog is dirty (check the dog's belly), then it is time for a bath.

2. It smells doggy. Some dogs, as mentioned above, have naturally strong odors. Most dogs, however, if given frequent brushing and clean sleeping quarters, remain sweet smelling for months at a

time. If you have been brushing your dog and keeping its sleeping quarters clean and it begins to smell, it is time for a bath. The bath will remove the skin bacteria which is causing the odor.

3. It has been skunked. Follow the directions in Chapter 8 under first aid. After the tomato juice bath, wash it with dog shampoo. Good luck.

4. It has been swimming in salt water. After a day at the beach, a dog should be bathed. The salt water cleans dirt off the dog, but the salt will cause itching and skin irritation.

HOW TO BATHE: When you have determined that your dog really needs a bath, it is wise to make the experience as comfortable as possible—for you and the dog. Some dogs love baths, some dogs tolerate them, some dogs think they are funny, and some dogs act as if every bath is a medieval torture. Juno, our female, is of the latter opinion. She simply hates baths, seems sure that she is going to drown in two inches of water, and cries, screams, and struggles throughout. Once her bath is over, she celebrates by breaking loose if she can and racing around our apartment, soaking everything and everyone. Since each of our dogs weighs approximately 100 pounds, we feel lucky that Arnold likes being bathed. If he didn't, we would need a rest cure several times a year.

Making your dog secure: Whatever your dog's attitude toward baths, it is a good idea to make it secure during bathing. Place a towel or a rubber mat on the bottom of the bathtub, sink, or laundry tub you have chosen as a dogtub. Fill the container with lukewarm (never hot or cold) water so that it will reach the dog's 'elbows.' Put the dog on the towel or mat so that its feet will not slip around. Some dogs become terrified when they can't get a firm footing.

Equipment: You will need some wads of sterilized cotton to put in the dog's ears (and your own if you have a dog like Juno) so water will not get into the inner ear. You will also need some petroleum jelly or mineral oil to put in and around the dog's eyes to protect them from soap. If you do not have a flexible shower hose, place a medium-sized metal pot with a handle near the tub. Also have on hand a clean sponge or a soft washcloth for washing the dog's face. Don't forget plenty of towels for drying.

Buy a good quality, mild dog shampoo. If your dog has fleas, use a

flea soap. *Never* use human soap or shampoo on a dog. It is too harsh for a dog's skin, and will cause dry skin problems and possible allergic reactions. In addition, the perfume in human shampoo and soap may please you, but it will irritate your dog's sensitive nose. If you perfume your dog, it is apt to roll in something which it feels is wonderful and you feel is foul—such as raccoon or cow dung.

If you wish, you can check with your vet to see if he wants to recommend a shampoo which is best for your dog.

Hair in the drain: To prevent hair from clogging the drain, have a piece of cheesecloth or some steelwool ready to place over or in the drain when the water is running out. Either material will catch the dog hairs before they clog your plumbing.

Method:

1. Gently rub the petroleum jelly or mineral oil on the dog's eyelids and around its eyes. If some gets in the eyes, that's all right. It will protect your dog's eyes from the soap. Put some cotton in each ear.

2. Place the dog on the towel or mat in the tub. There should be enough water in the tub to reach up to the dog's 'elbows.'

3. Using the flexible hose or the pot, thoroughly wet the dog to the skin. Be particularly thorough with long-haired dogs with double coats. Make sure that the belly of the dog and the ruff and the tail are wet.

4. Apply the shampoo. If you are using flea soap, begin by applying it around the head and the neck. This will prevent the fleas from escaping into the dog's ears.

5. Rub the soap in with your fingers and lather it well. Make sure that you lather the tail, the belly, the legs and the paws of your dog as well as the back and the sides. Massage the skin with the lather; that's where much of the dirt is.

6. Use the sponge or wash cloth to clean the dog's face and outer ear area.

7. Drain off the soapy water. Using the pot or the flexible hose, rinse the dog thoroughly with lukewarm water. Use your hands to work out the soap. Make sure the dog's belly is thoroughly rinsed. Soap left on the skin will cause dry skin and itching.

8. Dogs are very good at shaking water off their bodies. If you want to prevent a room from getting soaked, drape one of the towels over the dog's body and let it shake. Or, if you are working in a bathtub, you can close the shower curtain or doors and let the dog shake off the water. Then, using as many towels as necessary, give the dog a rubdown.

9. Most dogs will still be damp after a bath and rubdown. Have a place where they can settle and finish drying off or, if you wish, you can finish the job by using a hair dryer. Use a hand–held dryer or the hose from a cap dryer. Hold either at least ten inches from the dog.

10. Wipe off the excess petroleum jelly or mineral oil with a soft cloth.

11. Some dogs must relieve themselves right after a bath. If you have such a dog, don't let it out in a yard alone. Dogs have an annoying habit of rolling in dirt to complete the bathing routine. Supervise your dog's walk and then bring it indoors to dry off. Try not to bathe your dog in cold weather—except in emergencies. If you must give a cold weather bath, keep the dog out of all drafts for a few hours. If the dog has to relieve itself, wrap a dry towel around it and make it a very quick walk.

12. Never brush a wet or damp dog. Medium or long-haired dogs

will lose too much hair if you brush them wet. It will snaggle and come out in handfuls.

13. Don't bathe very young pups unless it is an emergency (i.e., skunking). If a young pup arrives from the kennel or pound in a smelly, filthy condition, thoroughly sponge it with a damp, soapless cloth. Clean the dirt off the skin on its belly with mineral oil and wads of cotton.

WATERLESS BATHS: You can buy spray foams, powdered shampoos, and cedar sawdust to be used as 'dry baths.' These products are rubbed into the coat and then brushed out.

Since frequent brushing and combing will keep a dog's coat clean and doggy odor is caused by dirty skin, we see no point in using these products. When your dog really needs a bath, give him one— water, soap, and scrubbing—from the skin out. If all he needs is a brushing, do it—without any fancy products.

EARS: Because many new dog owners never think of looking into their dog's ears, about 60 percent of the dogs we see have dirty, clogged, or infected ears. You should check your dog's ears once a

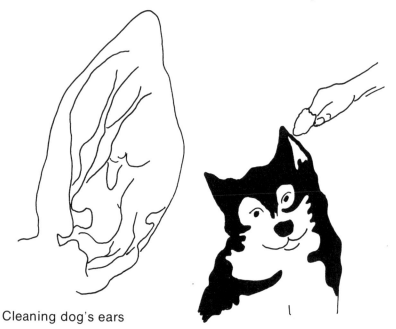

Cleaning dog's ears

week. First stick your nose next to the opening of each ear—if you smell a sour odor, go to a veterinarian. A bad smell is a sign of infection.

Look for dirt and grime on the tip of the ear and for dirty, waxy deposits in the inner ear. You will have to clean these away.

Equipment: You will need several wads of sterilized cotton and a bottle of mineral oil. NEVER use alcohol, peroxide, or cotton swabs in a dog's ears. Alcohol and peroxide dry up natural oils, and cotton swabs are too dangerous.

Method: Dip a wad of cotton into the mineral oil. Squeeze off any excess oil. Wrap the cotton around your index finger. Gently clean out the dog's ears. There are many crevices in a dog's ear, so check visually to see if you are reaching all of the waxy dirt. *Clean only what you can see.* Never probe deeply into a dog's ears to the non-visible parts. If you have let this cleaning go too long and you suspect that your dog has a clogged inner ear, see a vet.

Clean the dirt off the skin near the tip of the ear with more mineral oil and cottom.

Warning: Change the cotton wads frequently. Never use cotton from one ear to clean the other ear. If your dog has an infection or an ear parasite, this is a sure way to spread it.

HAIR IN EARS: Some breeds have so much hair in their inner ears that it tends to get matted. Instead of protecting the inner ear, this matted hair traps dirt and moisture. If you have such a dog, ask your vet to show you how to keep this hair trimmed.

CROPPED EARS: Breeders or veterinarians crop (cut and then tape) the ears of some breeds (for example, Boxers, Danes, Dobermans) when they are puppies. Usually these dogs have naturally long, floppy ears which, when left uncropped, protect the inner ears from dirt and grime. Many dogs with cropped ears have less protective hair in their inner ears than dogs with ears that naturally stand erect. If you have a dog with cropped ears and little protective hair, be extra diligent about checking the ears for dirt and waxy build-up.

EYES: Most healthy dogs do not need regular eye care. However, man has developed some breeds in such a way that regular eye care is necessary. This is particularly true of dogs having protruding eyes, such as Miniature Toy Poodles, Cocker Spaniels, and Lhasa Apsos.

These dogs often have eye discharges which get crusty, hard and mat the hair on their faces. If you have such a dog and your vet has told you that there is no eye infection, you should regularly (once a day) wipe off the discharge with some cotton and a mild boric acid solution or some mineral oil. This only takes a minute if done daily. If you have waited to do this and a build-up has occured, dip the cotton in mineral oil or a boric acid solution and soak the hardened discharge until it is soft enough to wipe away.

Some dogs with protruding eyes and long hair must have the hair combed away from their faces to prevent infection. Some dogs have very sensitive eyes and must have the hair combed over their eyes as a sun shield. Check a breed book for pictures. The standard grooming for a breed usually takes these physiological necessities into account.

EYES, EARS, AND AUTOMOBILES: We know that some people think it's cute to see the smiling faces of dogs hanging out of car windows. Many dogs love looking at the world go by at high speeds while the fifty or sixty mile an hour wind whips their faces. Unfortunately, it is dangerous.

A cinder or dust blown into a dog's eye at even thirty miles an hour can blind it. Dirt and dust forced into a dog's inner ears can cause infection. You can ride with the windows of your car open, but secure the dog with the leash attached to its leather collar so it can't stick its head into the wind. You will also be preventing it from jumping out of a moving car.

TEETH: Check your dog's teeth about once a month. Look for tartar build up near the gums and any suspicious dark spots. Discolored (yellowish) teeth are usually a sign that the dog was administered antibiotics when it was young. If your dog has problems chewing or shakes its head a lot, or if its face swells, it may have a toothache. See a vet.

If you feed your dog dry kibble, dog biscuits and an occasional beef leg bone, it will not get a tartar build-up on its teeth. Dogs raised on soft canned food, semi-soft food and table scraps tend to develop dental problems. If your dog now has a bad tartar problem near its gums because you didn't know how to prevent it or check for it, see your vet; he is also a dog dentist.

SHEDDING: Shedding is a normal physiological function. Humans are also constantly losing old dead hair and growing new hair. The ancestors of our dogs had a seasonal shedding pattern. They grew thick coats for the winter and shed them in the spring and summer. Modern dogs' biological clocks are a little haywire. With indoor heating, artificial light (animals' bodies respond to long and short days) and air conditioning, most dogs shed lightly year round.

Some breeds shed lightly year round and also shed heavily in the spring and, for females, after they have been in season or have given birth. The only solution to shedding is regular grooming.

NAILS: A dog's paw is an arrangement of four flexible, strong toes and five tough pads. A dog which is walking properly, should be walking squarely on these pads. If a dog's toenails are too long, the dog will be putting some of its weight on the nails. This will push the paws back at an uncomfortable angle and will, in time, cause painful problems for the animal.

If left unattended, a dog's nails can become ingrown. This is a particularly common problem with the dewclaw nail (the extra toe which grows above the front paw on dogs). Since the dewclaw never touches the ground during walking, its nail does not get worn down. Some breeds have their dewclaws removed just after birth, but most dogs, especially small ones, must have all nails groomed.

It is commonly believed that dogs which spend most of their lives walking on pavement do not require nail care. This is not true. Pavement does a certain amount of paring of nails for the dog but not enough. Small dogs in particular do not have the body weight to make the pavement act as a file. As one walks down a city street, one can hear the clicking of small dogs' nails on the pavement. Dogs should walk silently. If you can hear their nails click against the floor or pavement, it is time for a manicure.

A dog's nail has a vein and a nerve in it. The vein grows about three-fourths of the length of the nail. The nail surrounds the vein. If a dog's nails are kept short, the tiny veins stay short. If a dog's nails are allowed to grow uncontrolled, the veins and nerves keep growing.

If you have let your dog's nails get much too long, you will have to slowly shorten them—a fraction of an inch every few days. As you do this, the veins and the nerves will recede. If your dog's nails are already ingrown, take it to a vet.

FILING OR CLIPPING:

Equipment: A dog nail file or a dog nail clipper.
Method: Begin clipping or filing your puppy's nails when it is very young, even if you only have to remove one-sixteenth of an inch of nail. Have the pup lie on its side and sit next to it talking quietly and clipping or filing.

If you decide to file your dog's nails, do only a couple of nails at a sitting. Check to see if you can see the vein and leave some space between it and the tip of the nail. Filing a dog's nails should be painless. If the dog yelps, you have gotten too close to the nerve. Comfort the dog and go on to another nail.

Before you clip a dog's nails, check to see where the vein is. If your dog has dark nails, only clip a tiny portion of the nail off. Wait a few days and then clip some more.

If you make a mistake during nail clipping and blood appears on the nail, don't panic. Comfort the dog and apply some first aid

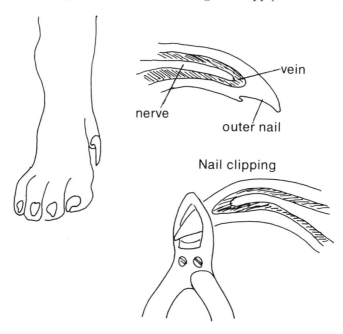

vein

nerve

outer nail

Nail clipping

cream or spray to the tip of the nail. Apply some pressure to the wound using a piece of cotton. The nail will stop bleeding within sixty seconds.

Don't let a mistake deter you. The emergency nail surgery that is performed on dogs who have never had their nails clipped or filed is far more painful than the one or two mistakes you might make. If you are really squeamish, use a file instead of a clipper—there will be fewer accidents.

If your dog absolutely will not sit still for a nail filing or clipping (perhaps you began doing this late in the dog's development), feed it one-fourth to one-half can of *flat* beer before you begin the clipping or filing. The malt in the beer is good for the dog, and the alcohol will settle the dog down. If you use beer, do all of the nails at once.

BURRS: If your dog gets a burr in its coat, soak the burr in petroleum jelly or mineral oil and then work it out with your fingers. Only cut it out as a last resort, if soaking does not work.

PAINT: Remove paint with mineral oil. Don't use turpentine on a dog; it irritates the skin and can poison a dog if licked. Mineral oil is a slower, less thorough process but it works.

CHEWING GUM AND TAR: If your dog has walked or rolled in chewing gum or tar, you will have to remove it from the dog's coat or from between the dog's toes. Hold an ice cube to the tar or gum. When it hardens, work it out. If it is really stuck between the toes, pour some mineral oil on the tar or gum after you harden it with ice, and work it away from the foot with your fingers.

FLEAS, TICKS, SKIN IRRITATIONS: As you groom your dog, look for parasites and skin irritations. Check the chapter on health to see what to do.

A FINAL WORD ABOUT GROOMING: Your dog's appearance says a lot about you and how you feel about him. If you're the sort of person who puts things off, your Old English Sheep Dog (or similar breed) is going to wind up looking like a brillo pad. There is no such thing as a breed that requires no grooming.

12. PUPPY KINDERGARTEN

There are two reasons why every puppy should be trained. Training makes a puppy easier to live with, and training makes having a puppy more fun for you.

Elsewhere in the book we talk about a few of the annoying habits that puppies develop and how to cure them. Our experience has shown us again and again that puppies who are receiving the formal training outlined in this chapter are *much* easier to break of bad habits than puppies who are trained in a piecemeal fashion—each problem undertaken separately. Very often behavior problems go away by themselves during the course of Puppy Kindergarten and obedience training.

In training your dog, you are teaching it specific responses to certain words. You are also teaching it that it will receive praise and approval for certain behavior. It may not seem very important to you that your puppy learns to walk precisely beside your left leg and sit automatically whenever you stop. It isn't important in itself. What is important is that the puppy is learning to watch you, to wait for your signal, and to understand exactly what you expect of it.

Many dog trainers still believe that a puppy should be at least six months of age before it begins formal training. We believe that six months is almost too late to begin if you want to raise a superpuppy.

You can begin your puppy kindergarten classes as soon as your puppy is settled in your home, after about forty-eight hours. You can begin with puppies as young as six weeks old.

Each lesson you give your puppy should last from five to ten minutes—no more. When the pup reaches fourteen weeks of age, you can increase the lessons to ten or fifteen minutes. By the time your puppy is four and a half months old, if you began early enough and worked diligently with the pup, it can be fully trained in the whole puppy kindergarten routine.

As you read this chapter and as you train your puppy, remember that it is a baby. Its attention span is short. It will often get bored or restless. When this happens, end the lesson. If you find that you have the time and the puppy is enjoying itself, give it two short lessons a day. If you find yourself losing your temper or getting impatient (there will be days when the sweetest puppy gets obstinate), stop the lesson. Your puppy can be a good friend. It can enjoy working for you and learning new things. Don't try to make it into a perfect robot. If you want a dog that always does everything correctly, get a wind-up toy and find another home for your living puppy.

LEASH TRAINING: No pup is born knowing how to walk on a leash. Too many people slip the new collar on the new puppy's neck, snap on the new leash and take a brisk walk around the neighborhood—dragging the puppy behind them. When the puppy sits or lies down on the pavement, refuses to move and begins to cry, it is either laughed at or called stupid. It is not stupid for a dog (or a person) to be frightened by a strange new experience. How would you feel if someone, twenty times your size, suddenly slapped a collar around your neck and began pulling you around? In order to avoid this kind of trauma and to create, instead, happy associations with the leash and collar, do the following:

1. When the puppy gets somewhat comfortable in your home, put on the leather collar. Let the pup get used to it. Leave any tags off the collar for the first few days; no need to confuse the pup with sound (tags jingle) in addition to the feel of the collar. If the puppy tries to scratch the collar off, distract it with play and treats and petting. Make sure that the collar is not too tight.

2. When the puppy seems to be comfortable wearing the collar

(this can take anywhere from ten minutes to twenty-four hours, depending upon the dog), attach the leash and let the puppy drag it around for about ten minutes (in a fenced yard or indoors). Stay with the pup during this time to prevent it from tangling, chewing, or urinating on the leash.

3. When the pup seems comfortable dragging around the leash, pick up the end of the leash. Let the puppy lead you around for ten minutes. If the pup seems tired, end the lesson here. If not, continue to Step 4.

4. Hold the end of the leash. Begin walking. Do not drag the puppy. Call to the puppy, encourage it, pat the side of your leg; if it refuses to move in your chosen direction, give the leash several gentle but firm tugs. Keep calling to the pup, walking and, if necessary, gently tugging. If you have been indoors during all of this, go outside if the weather permits.

Never force the pup to walk up or down stairs while you are dragging it on a leash. See "Bringing Your Puppy Home" for instructions regarding stairs.

5. When the puppy has rested (perhaps the next day), take a walk with it around the neighborhood on the leash. Keep encouraging the pup, gently tugging on the leash and saying, "goooood dog." Bend over and pet the pup whenever possible. Comfort it if it gets frightened. If it seems terribly frightened and is shaking from nervousness, take it inside and give it another short walk later in the day. It is very important to slowly introduce nervous dogs to leash walking on the street. However, do not spoil such a dog. It is important that you help the nervous animal gain confidence, or you will wind up with a grown dog which refuses to leave the house and is terrified of all new and strange situations and people.

Do not allow your pup to roll over and refuse to move. It is better to end a walk and begin the leash lesson another day or at a later hour than to get your dog used to being carried all of the time. Small dogs are especially good at conning their owners into carrying them. Dogs need exercise; make your pup walk, gently but firmly. Remember it is a baby and will probably get tired easily. If you are working with a very young puppy, don't go on any long leash walks with it for a while.

Later in puppy kindergarten you will teach your pup to heel (walk on your left side).

THE TRAINING SCHEDULE: Puppies work and learn at different paces, just like humans. It is possible to bully a puppy into learning quickly but it is really best to go slow and easy with young animals. Make yourself a schedule and keep a record of the times you are training your pup, the specific skills you are teaching it and the pup's progress. You may find that some skills take only a few days to teach your puppy and some take a week or two. Never go on to a new skill until you are sure that your puppy knows the old skills. If you get discouraged, look back at your training schedule and check to see the progress your puppy has made. Keep reminding yourself that you are teaching a being that has only been alive for six, eight, or ten weeks.

SIGNALS: During training, your puppy will be learning three kinds of signals—verbal (voice), physical (placing him where he should be), and visual (hand and foot signals). It is very important that you control the tone of your voice so that it is always kind, happy, and firm. Never shout at your pup and don't nag at it. When it does something right, even if you had to tell it something five times and then place it in the right position, remember to praise it with "goooood dog" and some nice petting.

When you begin using hand signals, do them exactly the same way each time. Since the puppy will eventually be watching your legs as well as your hands, always begin on the proper foot for moving exercises. Training a dog is a bit like riding a bicycle or learning to ice skate. You may feel awkward at first but practice makes the process easier and, finally, much fun.

SIT AND STAND (WEEK ONE): After your puppy knows what a leash and a collar are for, it will be ready to learn "sit" and "stand." We advise that you teach your puppy stand. It is necessary for obedience competitions and show rings, and is a very useful aid to grooming and bathing any dog. Stand is a helpful command to give a dog on a muddy, rainy day when it wants to sit in a puddle, and it is handy during veterinarian visits.

There is only one big "don't" involved with these exercises. Don't put pressure on any puppy's hindquarters to make it sit. Dogs have the ability to lock their four legs into a standing position. The harder you push down, the more they tense their muscles. You will probably win the battle, but you do not want to fight your puppy—you want to train it. In addition, many dogs are susceptible to hip dysplasia. Pressure on the hips does them no good at all.

SIT: Kneel down and place the puppy on your left side. Slip your right hand under the puppy's collar. Say, "Brutus, sit" and scoop the puppy's rear into a sitting position using your left hand. Move your left hand away. Pet the dog with your left hand and say, "goooood Brutus."

STAND: Then slip your left hand, palm down, under the pup's belly. Say, "Stand" (no name here). Gently raise the dog onto its feet. Say, "goooood Brutus. Stand, goooood Brutus, stand."

Then repeat the sit exercise and the stand exercise. Do this for about five minutes the first day.

On the second day, give the command, wait a few seconds to see if the puppy does it, and then help it into position. Praise. During practice for the next few days, give the puppy a chance to sit or stand without physical help before you place it. Keep this up in five to ten-minute lessons each day until the puppy really knows both commands. These are the first human words the pup is learning. Be patient.

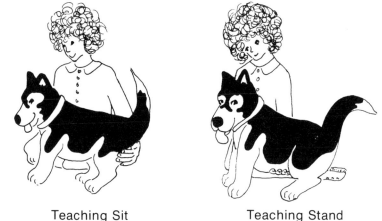

Teaching Sit   Teaching Stand

As soon as your puppy knows these two words, begin giving it the commands while you are standing next to it (pup on your left side). Leash the puppy. If it does not sit, give the leash a gentle tug upwards and say, "no, sit". Then praise. If the pup does not stand, help it up with your hands and then praise.

STAY (WEEK TWO): You should begin teaching "stay" only after your puppy knows sit and stand. Teach the sit-stay and the stand-stay in a quiet place—indoors or in an enclosed yard. Once your puppy knows the meaning of the words, you can begin practicing the stays on the sidewalk, on busy shopping streets and in playgrounds.

SIT-STAY:

1. Leash your puppy. Have the pup sit next to your left side (you are standing). Hold the end of the leash in your right hand.

2. Place your left hand, palm toward the pup, in front of the puppy's nose. Tell the dog to "stay", firmly but gently.

3. Grab the middle of the leash with your left hand. Hold your left hand (with the leash in it) over the pup's head and take a very small step to the right.

4. Count to two and step back next to the pup. Bend over and give a gentle pat to the pup. Say "gooood dog," very calmly.

If the pup gets up while you are taking your step away from it, give the leash a gentle jerk straight upwards and say "no, sit—stay." If the pup has moved, place it in the exact spot where it began and begin again.

Repeat the entire exercise—only work your way around the pup with each new leave-taking. Always give both the hand signal and the command "stay" before you leave. Always leave with your right foot. Always return to the pup so that it is on your left side. Always praise the pup when you return.

As your puppy learns the word stay, you can begin staying away for longer periods of time (count to five and then ten and then twenty). When the puppy gets good at staying, begin to move farther away from it until you can stand at the end of the leash while the pup stays for at least thirty seconds.

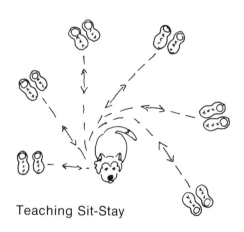

Teaching Sit-Stay

Do not drop the leash and walk away, no matter how good the puppy seems to be. Do not give the command stay in the house while the pup is off the leash. Off the leash work is part of more advanced obedience. If your puppy realizes that it can get up and wander away when no leash is attached to it, you are going to have problems later on.

STAND-STAY: Stand-stay is a difficult exercise for an energetic puppy. Your puppy will probably do much better at first with the sit-stay. During this week of practice, work for at least two minutes of each session on stand-stay. Spend the rest of the time on sit-stay.

1. Place your pup on your left side. Tell it to stand.

2. Place your right hand on its chest below its chin. Place your left hand on the inside of its right rear leg. Say, "Stay".

3. Remove your left hand. If the pup looks as if it is going to sit down, calmly say "no, stand, stay" and put your left hand back on the inside of the rear leg. Say, "stay" and remove the left hand.

4. When the pup remains standing, gently remove your right hand from its chest. Say, "stay."

Teaching Stand-Stay

5. If the pup walks forward, replace your right hand on its chest and say "no, stay." Keep saying, "stand, stay, goooood dog", softly.

As your puppy becomes steady with the stand-stay, you can begin moving away from it a bit after giving the command. Always give the hand signal when you move away from it. Always leave on your right foot. Work on it so you can walk to the end of the leash, stand there for ten or fifteen seconds and return while the puppy stands absolutely still.

Never let the puppy sit down when you return to it. Return to the puppy, count to three and then walk forward, starting with your *left* foot, calling to the pup. Say "O.K." to signal that the exercise is over. Pet the dog.

When your puppy is really doing solid sit-stays and stand-stays, begin giving the commands only once, with the signal for stay. Only repeat the commands, with the word "no," if the pup begins to move.

DOWN (WEEK THREE): Down is a command which is often resisted by dogs, despite the fact that they spend much of their lives lying down. Be sure that your puppy really knows sit-stay and stand-stay before you begin down. Be extra gentle during the teaching of down and never, never give the command without making the dog do it.

1. First of all, whenever you see your dog lie down during this week of training, say "goooood dog, down." This may seem a little underhanded, but it will help teach the word.

2. Kneel next to your puppy, pup on your left side. Tell the pup to sit.

3. Reach over your puppy with your left arm and gently take the pup's left front leg in your left hand. Gently shake the leg up and down until the paw is floppy and relaxed.

4. Then take the right front leg in your right hand and shake it until the right paw is floppy and relaxed.

5. When both paws are loose and relaxed, say, "Down." Tap the floor with your right hand, directly in front of the pup. Some pups will slide into a down position at this point. If your pup does this

Teaching Down

give it an enthusiastic "goooood dog, down" and a nice back rub. If not:

6. Gently ease the puppy down by sliding its relaxed front paws forward. Keep saying, "down, goooood dog, down."

7. When it is lying down, stroke its whole back and keep repeating the word "down". Mix in a number of "goooood dogs."

8. Tell the puppy to sit and begin again.

Don't expect the puppy to remain lying down for long. Down-stay is the next lesson. If your puppy chooses to lie on its back, fine. Down simply means to lie down. If you want it lying down on its stomach, don't give it a belly rub when it rolls over during the lesson. Save the belly rubs for play time.

After the puppy seems to know the word down, begin standing next to it and giving the command. As you do this, raise your right arm up for the formal down signal. If the pup doesn't lie down, bring your right arm down and gently slap the leash in a downward motion, and repeat the command. If it still doesn't lie down, place it down. Praise and pet your puppy.

You will now be practicing sit-stay, stand-stay and down during each lesson. The lessons will have to be a bit longer. Mix up the exercises—some sit-stay, some down, some sit-stay, some stand-stay—keep it interesting for the puppy. Give the pup a play break half way through. Give it a chance to relieve itself. Practice the stay exercises in busy places. Have a good romp with the puppy at the end of each lesson.

DOWN-STAY (WEEK FOUR): Your puppy already knows sit-stay, stand-stay, and down. Down-stay is going to be easy.

1. Leash the pup. Place it at your left side, sitting. Give it the down hand signal and say "down." If it doesn't lie down, correct it gently with the downward slap on the leash.

2. Hold the end of the leash in your right hand. Let the rest of the leash hang loose.

3. Give the stay signal and the stay command to the puppy. Take a small step to your right. Count to three. Return to your dog. Praise.

4. If your puppy gets up, return it to the spot where it started, tell it down, and begin again.

Down hand signal

Down correction

5. Repeat this exercise again, stepping with your right foot a little behind the pup. Do it in the exact same way you did the sit-stay exercise.

6. As with the sit-stay, work until you can stand at the end of the leash for thirty seconds while the dog remains on a down-stay.

Do not do down-stay off the leash. Do not let the dog sit when you return to it—until you tell it to. You should now be practicing sit-stay, stand-stay and down-stay during each lesson. Mix in some sits without stays and downs without stays and some leash walking. The most difficult thing for a puppy is to remain relatively immobile for ten to fifteen minutes. Give it a little break.

COME (WEEK FIVE): Puppies love this exercise. If you never scold or punish your puppy when you call it and if you do this exercise properly, you will be conditioning your pup to come to you, no matter what it is doing, whenever it hears "Brutus come." Coming to you (also known as the Recall) should be the most joyous event in your pup's life. If it knows that 25 percent of the times you call it, it is going to get scolded, it is going to make a decision to run in the opposite direction when it hears your voice.

1. From now on, you may call your puppy to you whenever you want to but say, "here, Brutus" or "let's go, Brutus." The only time you will use the formal command "Brutus, come" is when your puppy is leashed. You are going to condition it to drop everything and show up for that formal combination of words. Later on, when you get to off-leash work, you will be able to learn how to enforce the "Brutus, come" from a distance. Now you are laying a foundation for that advanced work.

2. Leash your puppy. Put it on a sit-stay and go to the end of the leash directly in front of the dog.

3. Hold the leash in your left hand. Place your right hand out to the side, shoulder level, palm facing the dog. Bend the arm at the elbow and bring your hand toward your chest. While you are doing this say "Brutus come" in your happiest, nicest voice.

4. As the dog comes toward you, kneel down, gather up the leash and keep saying, "Brutus, come."

Teaching Come

5. When it gets close to you, pet it and make it sit directly in front of you. Give much praise.

6. Put the dog on another sit-stay. Go to the end of the leash. *Return to your dog.* Leave it on a sit-stay again. This time, call it. It is very important that you keep mixing up this exercise. Do not call your dog everytime you put it on a stay. Call it only about 40 percent of the time. If you call it every time, it will anticipate you and stop staying. It will try to go to you each time it sees you get to the end of the leash.

If your pup does not come when you say "Brutus, come," bring your right hand down and gently tap the leash. This will get the pup on its feet moving.

When your puppy gets really good at come, begin giving the command from a standing position without kneeling down at all. Gather the leash in as the pup gets close. Make it sit in front of you and then bend over and praise it with lots of ear rubbing and "gooooood dog."

Each lesson now includes sit, sit-stay, stand-stay, down, down-stay, and come.

HEEL (WEEK SIX): Most puppies can be taught to heel using the leather collar and a training leash. If your puppy is very energetic or, perhaps, very large, it will need a chain collar (training collar) and some basic obedience work in this area. Try this technique first on young puppies. Your puppy already knows so much that it might surprise you in the heeling exercise.

1. Leash your puppy on its leather collar. Have it sit by your left side.

2. Hold the end of the leash in your right hand. Grab the middle of the leash in your right hand, too. Place your left hand on the leash near the pup's collar.

3. Keep the leash slack. The puppy should feel no pressure from the leash. Say, "Brutus, heel" in a cheerful voice.

4. As you say this, begin walking—*left* foot first. If the pup remains sitting, give the leash a little jerk and encourage the pup. Talk to it.

5. Keep walking. When the pup is right next to you on your left side, say "goooood dog." When it forges ahead, lags behind or veers off to the side, give the leash a little jerk and say "no, heel." Occasionally pat your left leg with your hand; keep talking to the pup and correcting it with jerks of the leash and telling it "goood dog, heel."

Correction for heel

6. Do not drag the pup around. When the puppy is heeling next to you, the leash should hang loose. It only gets jerked when the pup is wrong. It never should remain tight with the pup leaning into it.

7. Whenever you stop, slow down a bit first, come to a full stop and tell the dog to sit. Praise the dog. Make sure it is sitting next to your left leg.

8. As your dog gets better at this, you will find that you will be giving fewer and fewer corrections (jerks) with the leash. You will also find that the puppy is sitting automatically whenever you stop.

Heeling is the most difficult part of dog training for the human involved. You will probably feel a bit awkward at first. You'll get dizzy from watching the puppy to make sure you don't trip on it. As you get more confident, you will find that you can sense just where the puppy is and are able simply to walk at a normal pace, giving corrections when needed.

Practice heeling at different paces. Walk very slow as if the ground were icy and also trot with the pup. As the pup and you get comfortable with heeling, have the dog heel a bit on every walk. We don't believe that a puppy should be on duty and working at all times so give it a break—use the word "easy." Tell the pup easy and let it sniff around and wander at the end of the leash without pulling. Then make it heel some more.

Now, each session, you are going to be practicing everything you and the pup learned together. When you feel that your puppy is doing well on all exercises, you might want to join an obedience club to learn some advanced work. If you don't want to do this, continue practicing at least three times a week with your puppy for a few months—to sharpen the work and to keep the pup busy. However, superpuppies often get bored with kindergarten work and really need more advanced work to keep their minds busy. If you've done this much in such a short time, think of all your pup could learn if given a chance. Good luck.

13. PROBLEM SOLVING AND PROBLEM PREVENTION

A well-trained dog is easy to live with. It understands what is expected of it. It knows its place in the family, its privileges and responsibilities. A well-trained dog is secure. It knows the rules and boundaries of life with its human family. Imagine driving a car in a foreign country with no idea of the speed limit, the laws of traffic, the penalties for breaking laws you don't even know about—you wouldn't feel secure until you found out the rules. Your dog needs to know what's permitted, and what's not. Well-trained dogs are happy, because they feel secure, and have something to accomplish and feel proud about.

A trained dog is apt to have better judgment that he would not have developed without having been trained. He understands that his conduct is governed by rules, and he can often apply those rules to new situations—or at least consider that a new situation might have a rule applying to it that he doesn't know about. For example: Juno killed a mouse last night which is not her regular job. There just happened to be a mouse in our work room, and Juno did it in. We found Juno standing over her mouse, looking apprehensive. She knows that there is a rule about mauling small animals (cats) but instinct had directed her to kill the mouse. Now she was clearly waiting for a ruling. We told her that she had done well; Juno looked confused. She appeared to think it over, and then snapped at a cat, got scolded, and seemed relieved. It seems that she was testing the new policy, which permits her to kill small animals (mice), but not certain specific small animals (cats). We can't be sure that Juno was really thinking all this out, but what is evident about all of Juno's conduct is that she understands that anything she does or wants to do is subject to our approval. In the case of the mouse, it was clear to us, from Juno's manner and past experience, that she was perfectly willing to be instructed not to kill mice, if that was our desire. It isn't, but it would have been easy enough. Saying, "No! Bad!" sternly would probably have done the trick, permanently. As it is, we let matters stand, and Juno has gone into partnership with one of the cats. They have staked out the mousehole, and if another mouse ever comes in here, woe to him.

Some methods of training are less apt to develop any sort of independent judgment in the dog. The object of some methods is to make the dog instantly obedient to certain commands, like a soldier on parade. This kind of training doesn't interest us. We happen to think that dogs can reason after a fashion, and we like to give them a chance to develop that skill to its highest possible level.

Some people feel that housebreaking is the only requirement a dog has to meet. We feel that housebreaking is only one of three basic *musts* in dog owning. The others are 2) never bite and 3) never run out into traffic. These are common sense rules: nobody likes to live with a dog's filth, not even the dog; a dog that bites is a menace; and being hit by a car is a preventable tragedy.

To really enjoy living with a dog, you should go beyond these three basics. The dog is more than willing to learn much more sophisticated rules of conduct. All you have to do is be willing to teach it with patience, fairness, and consistency.

EXPECTATIONS: We have said before that a puppy will sense what you want, and try its best to provide it—another way of saying that you will probably wind up with the dog you deserve. If you get a sick thrill out of a dog that growls and snaps at people, it will be very difficult to teach it not to use its teeth. If you like the idea of your pup begging at the table, you will never be truly successful at preventing it, unless your true feelings change. And remember, anything the dog does as a puppy, it is apt to do as an adult.

Some people expect their puppy to learn a new rule, skill, or trick the first time it is taught. Puppies are babies; even young human beings need special consideration when they first begin to learn things. Teaching a young puppy takes patience, consistency and calm. You will meet people with stories about how old Shep only had to be told a thing once, and never forgot it. These dogs tend to be very old, or dead. Their owners don't remember the effort the dog's early training required. There may be pups who never make the same mistake twice, but they are as rare as humans who never make the same mistake twice. If you've got one, congratulations. You are a lucky person, especially if you plan to never have another dog when your genius dies. If you do, be prepared for a lot of patient, consistent, calm work.

Most puppies have to be shown a new skill a number of times, in *exactly the same way each time*. Puppies will sometimes forget and make mistakes. They will sometimes get stubborn. They will sometimes get bored (their attention span is short). They will have spells of silliness, and many will out-and-out defy you at times.

Expect great things from your puppy, but temper these expectations with humor, patience, and love. No puppy can be 100 percent perfect while it is learning. Every time you shout at your pup, lose your temper, or hit it out of frustration, you confuse it, and undo the very work you are trying to accomplish.

PRAISE AND CORRECTION: Praise is going to be your puppy's paycheck. If you praise your puppy with a muttered "good dog," and a small pat on the head, it will work accordingly—with slight enthusiasm. If you praise your puppy by saying, "Gooood dog!" and give it a good ear rub, it will work with pleasure and spirit. Dogs love hammy acting. They are good actors themselves, and they appreciate it in others. If you want to tell your dog that he has pleased you—overdo it!. If you are a quiet, undemonstrative person, you had better change all that, as far as your dog is concerned.

It is not a good idea to bribe your puppy with treats during training. If you use bribes to train your dog, he is apt to go on strike the

first time you run out of yummies. Besides, it seems a little silly to make a mercenary pieceworker out of an animal who is perfectly willing to work as hard as he can for praise and respect from his human friend. You can give your dog a treat, as an extra, *after* the lesson is over.

There will be times in your puppy's life when it will require punishment. A light slap on the nose with two fingers when the pup tries to nip or chew on a human is the *ONLY* time we sanction hitting a dog. It isn't just that hitting can get out of control. It doesn't work, and that includes hitting with a rolled up newspaper. All you can teach a dog by continually hitting it is to fear you.

There are a number of other ways to control your puppy, and even punish it when necessary, that work better than slamming it around. You have already read in the housebreaking section about isolation as a punishment. We will go over it again here.

ISOLATION: This is the most effective punishment we know of. There are two rules about it: 1) The puppy must have done something serious enough to deserve it, and 2) the puppy must know that he has done it, and that you are not in favor of his doing it again. This requires (preferably) catching him in the act, or showing him the damage just before punishment. There is no need to put on an angry act. In fact, even if you are angry, don't make a show of it. When someone breaks the law, a cop will arrest him. The cop doesn't have to act mad, or hate the person who may have made an illegal left turn in traffic. He broke a law, and he has to pay a penalty—there's no need to get emotional. Bear in mind that most dogs appreciate emotional scenes and look upon them as theater.

Find a spot where you can secure a short (about 18 inches) chain. This should be a part of the house that can be vacated by everyone, including the cat, during the puppy's isolation. After establishing what the puppy is being punished for (this is for the puppy's benefit), tie or clip the chain to the puppy's *leather* collar, and leave him for ten minutes. When you come back, forgive the puppy and start fresh. This is more effective than clobbering the dog with a newspaper.

Don't punish the pup when it is newly arrived in your home, and don't punish the pup for every little thing. A strong, "NO!" should do the trick for all but serious crimes.

PROBLEM PREVENTION AND PROBLEM SOLVING: Everything, every event and every experience in your puppy's life, will affect its education. If you allow problems to develop because you are lazy, or unsure of just what you will want from your puppy, you will have to solve them—and solving is harder than preventing. Decide beforehand what kind of "Person" you want your puppy to be. Plan to raise it in such a way that problems are prevented. If you begin by shouting at your puppy whenever you want to tell it something, you will condition it to respond only to shouted commands. If you talk quietly and gently to your pup, you will accustom it to listening carefully to quiet commands. A good rule to keep in mind is this: Anything your puppy is doing now, he is apt to do always. Decide which things you want to discourage.

HOUSEBREAKING: This is one of the *musts*. There's a whole chapter about it earlier in this book. Read it, and begin training your pup in his first days with you.

BEGGING: The best way to prevent a dog from annoying people while they eat is to make a simple rule: *No one may ever feed the puppy from the table.* This includes Aunt Hortense. If you allow guests or family members to break this rule, you will have a problem on your hands. Explain this to people who think it's cute to feed the dog scraps. They aren't doing him a favor, and they aren't making things any easier for you.

Feed the puppy at least half an hour before the family eats. If you do this, no one can feel sorry for the "poor starving beastie." It is not a good idea to feed the pup at the same time the family eats, because many pups will simply ignore their dinner, and wait around for some sympathy and people food.

Do not give the puppy scraps—even in its own dish, between courses. Two problems can be created by doing this. The first is a dog who is underfoot every time someone gets up from the table to remove dishes. The second is a dog who decides that as long as it is going to get snacks after each course, it may as well hang around the table and save wasted footsteps. If you are having something that would agree with your dog, save it up for *after* the meal. We know a very nice family who didn't pay attention to this matter.

Their puppy was a Great Dane, and sooner than anyone expected he was big enough to rest his chin on the table next to people's plates. Then the family decided to solve the problem they had created.

If your dog begs, stop all from-the-table and between-course snacking. Save the scraps, if you wish, and put them in the dog's dish *after* everyone has finished and the table has been cleared. Don't give the dog scraps at every meal; this is as much for the sake of good nutrition as training. Check the diet section in Chapter 9. When the dog bothers people at the table, push it away and tell it "No!" firmly. As you begin formal training, you can leash the dog, and tell it "Down-stay!" during meals, or you can say "Go to your room!"

Remember the lesson the Dane's family learned. A tiny puppy may seem cute when it begs—the same habit can be a nuisance in an adult.

DESTROYING PROPERTY: Puppies, even small ones, can do a great deal of damage with their teeth; they can chew up clothing, shoes, socks, furniture, and rugs. There are a number of reasons puppies engage in this activity, but no reason is an excuse to let them get away with it. Puppies chew your possesions because they are bored, or teething, or because they think it is fun, or out of spite or anger. All perfectly good reason, but bad excuses. Every puppy chews things; it is your business to make sure that they are not things of yours.

If you provide your pup with things that are more interesting to chew than your possesions, you will avoid a lot of sorrow. Puppies really like to sink their teeth into things, especially when they are teething. Soft rubber toys don't really provide a good substitute for chair legs or shoes. They are too soft, and don't taste as good to a puppy.

You can buy rawhide bones and toys for your pup as well as hard rubber toys. Even better are boiled beef leg bones (see Chapter 9 for method of preparation). Keep extra bones in the refrigerator or freezer. No pup we know ever preferred a piece of furniture to a fresh boiled beef leg bone. The following are ways to use the pup's toys and bones to prevent destruction:

1. Provide your pup with a number of toys—a tug toy, a hard rubber ball, an old towel, some rubber chew toys, as well as the good old bone. When you are at home with the pup, take up most of the toys, and put them out of reach. When you are ready to go out, put them *all* down just before you leave. If you are to be out for a number of hours, provide the pup with a fresh beef leg bone too. We don't do this with our grown dogs, and we hardly ever see them playing with their toys, which are all over the house, when we're home. But this afternoon when we came back from our puppy school, we found that some dog or dogs had assembled the entire bone collection (covering years), the green nylon bones, the rubber mice, the hard rubber toy that we've *never* seen them touch, the rubber hedgehog, all in a heap in the middle of the room. Apparently they were bored, and got up some sort of a game. If you leave your pup with all this clutter, it will have something to do. The bone is especially useful. It can chew on it if its gums begin to bother it, and if it is a fresh bone, the pup will work on it until exhausted, and fall asleep. Most dogs, pups and adults, sleep most of the time they are left alone in the house.

2. Beginning on the first day you have your new puppy, put it in a confined space, such as the kitchen, and leave it for a few minutes at a time. Go into another room, out of sight, and make no noise. Do this ten to fifteen times a day for the first few days the pup is with you. Gradually increase the time spent away from the pup. After a few days of this leave-taking, you can leave the house for periods of time. Combine longer periods of leave-taking with short periods. For example: Leave for five minutes, return and play with the pup; leave for ten minutes, return and play; for eight minutes; for fifteen minutes; for five minutes; for an hour. Don't just vanish. Say goodbye to the puppy, in exactly the same words you will use all its life. We say "Guard the house." During the puppy's first week with you, you should leave and return at least a hundred times.

This does several things for the puppy. It builds up confidence that you are always going to return when you leave. Looking at it from the point of view of a chewing pup, it also means that you might return at any time, thereby heading off spite chewing in two ways. It makes this behavior risky for the culprit; and it eliminates the main reason. Puppies and dogs who destroy property out of spite are getting even with their people for leaving them alone. These are usually animals which have spent all their time with humans. The first time they are left alone they throw a fit, after which it becomes a habit unless broken with human help.

3. Which leads us to the third step in chewing prevention. Even if someone—a mother or grandparent—will always be at home with the dog, practice leaving and returning. In fact, if the dog is to be with humans most of the time, it is even more important for the family to cooperate in the leave-taking exercise. There will be a day when everyone has to be out of the house at one time without the dog. Prevention is easier than cure, especially if the cure involves getting new rugs and a new leg for the dining-room table. When you are practicing the leave-taking, have most of the family leave the house, or keep them quiet. Don't have a group of people in the next room laughing or watching television while the pup is confined. That is punishment and not training.

4. Some people find that a puppy appreciates the sound of a radio when left alone for long periods. You can try this. Most dogs like talk stations, although some prefer music.

5. Some people prevent destructiveness caused by lonely dogs by getting the dog a pet such as a kitten, a fish, or a caged bird. Other living things regardless of size or shape make puppies less lonely. If your pup is to be left alone all day, five days a week, perhaps you can consider getting it a pet.

6. *Never* use a basement or garage as the place to keep your puppy when you are gone. Such places are too large, damp and frightening for a new puppy. Don't put your puppy in a tiny bathroom; it is too small and confining. A kitchen is usually the best place to confine a puppy until it is trained. If you have no kitchen door, construct some sort of temporary barrier out of plywood or the like. Once your pup is trained, it can have the run of the house.

7. If you come home and find the pup chewing on something forbidden, grab the pup by the leather collar, show it what it did, and say, "Bad dog!" in a firm voice. Then give it one of its own toys or bones, and say, "Gooood dog!"

If your puppy already has a bad chewing problem, try the leave-taking routine described above (step 2) but this time, come and go at least twenty-five to fifty times the first day. When you come in, come in fast. Do it again the next day. Combine it with taking up most of the toys when you are at home, and putting them down just before you begin the leave-taking exercise for the day.

If you catch your pup in the act of chewing, make a *very* big production of it, "Bad dog!" Make sure you are getting your message across. Always make a big production of leaving, saying goodbye to the dog, etc. When you return, come in like gangbusters. After a while, the pup is going to get the feeling that you've come back more times than you've left. Whenever the pup thinks of you, he will think of you as a person who is likely to burst through the front door any second. It is hard to get started chewing with thoughts like that. Besides, the puppy has a new hobby—watching the front door for his funny owner to come bursting in.

This takes a few days of boring activity, but it will save your possesions, cure a bad habit, and build up the puppy's security.

If the dog is sneaking into another room when you are home, and destroying property, use isolation as a punishment, each and every time he does it. Remember more than ten minutes in solitary is seldom called for.

If the leave-taking routine and/or isolation have not worked, even after you've given them both a chance (remember, pups learn at different rates—some have to do ten stretches in solitary before they catch on—here's another method. Buy a product called Grannick's Bitter Apple in a squeeze bottle. It is sold at pet supply stores (if you can't find it, check the back of the book for mail-order houses). When you catch the pup destroying something, or when you come home and find possesions destroyed, grab the pup by its leather collar, show it the damage, say "Bad dog!" and squirt *one* drop of Bitter Apple on its tongue. Then squirt some Bitter Apple on the object the pup has chewed. Then isolate the pup for ten minutes. Don't forget to forgive him afterwards!

Dogs hate the taste of Bitter Apple. You only have to use a drop or two at a time. The pup may foam at the mouth a bit after getting the Bitter Apple treatment, but it won't hurt him. Bitter Apple does not stain furniture and is odorless when dry—but the dog can smell it and taste it! When it goes to chew again, it will encounter the Bitter Apple and back off. The drop (only *one!*) on the pup's tongue is to give him an idea of what the stuff tastes like. You don't have to drown him in it. Try a drop on your own tongue, and you'll get the idea.

We have tried every dog repellent we could find—we even tried concocting our own—and Bitter Apple seems to be the best product for the job. It is also useful for keeping a dog from chewing or sucking his own fur, and to keep dogs from chewing bandages off.

If none of the above methods work, call a responsible dog trainer for advice. Before you look for help, think about whether you really tried—a fair number of times, using a single method. If you skip from one approach to another after a failure or two, you are being inconsistent, and not giving your dog a chance to learn.

JUMPING ON PEOPLE: A bad habit many dogs develop is jumping up on people as a greeting. They learn to do this when they are young because many people think it is playful and cute when a pup leaps in the air, dances around and paws at them with its front legs.

When a dog matures, this habit stops being so cute. An eighty pound Siberian Husky can knock a grown man to the floor by jumping. A four pound Chihuahua can rip slacks, stockings and bare skin with its claws. No dog should be allowed to get away with this behavior.

As the pup is growing up, *never* let it jump on people. As it jumps either back away fast or gently push it away and say "No", (Don't say "Down," that's going to mean something specific later). Do this every time it jumps. Have family and friends cooperate with you. Wrestle and play with the pup all you want, but don't allow jumping on people to be part of its fun.

If your pup is older, or if you have an older dog which has already developed the jumping habit, begin raising your knee and pushing the dog away with the knee, *every time* it jumps. *Do not* kick the dog.

If that doesn't seem to work, or if you find it uncomfortable for any reason, when the dog jumps grab one of its paws in each hand and firmly squeeze the toes together with a steadily increasing pressure, until the dog looks uncomfortable or yelps. Now you know how hard to squeeze the next time. Talk to the dog while you are doing this. It is not punishment, it is just a cop giving the dog a ticket for jumping in a "no jumping" zone. Do this *every* time it jumps.

BARKING: Some dogs like to bark all the time. Some dogs bark because they like the sound of their own voices, some dogs bark because they are bored, some dogs bark because they are lonely and want to attract attention, and some dogs simply begin barking and get so carried away that they find it difficult to stop. Any kind of constant barking is annoying to a dog's family and neighbors.

The prevention or cure of chronic barking both work the same way. They are both based on teaching the dog the word "quiet."

In order to teach the pup "Quiet!" you have to be around when the pup is making some noise. Buy a little squeeze bottle of lemon juice (they are usually shaped like plastic lemons). Keep the lemon juice handy. When the pup gets into a fit of barking, squirt a little lemon juice in its mouth (look out for the eyes!) and say "Quiet!" The lemon juice makes the puppy's mouth pucker, and it stops barking; "Gooood dog! Quiet! Goood dog!"

Only do this when you feel the pup should not be barking. *Never* provoke your dog to make it bark, and then give it lemon juice—that is teasing, not training.

It does not matter if your dog likes lemon juice (some do). This method is intended merely to quiet the pup, not punish it with a bad-tasting substance. The point of the exercise is that it is hard to bark with your mouth all puckered up. The pup will learn to associate the taste of lemon juice with the sight of the bottle, and then with the word "quiet" which you have been repeating with each administration of juice. Soon you will see your pup begin to pucker, and salivate (and stop barking) on the hearing the word, "quiet."

As soon as your dog knows the meaning of the word "quiet," stop using the lemon juice—just keep praising your dog whenever it stops barking on command. If the dog has a relapse, simply showing it the bottle will remind it of what "quiet" means.

If your dog is already a chronic barker, you should use this method, but you will have to do it more frequently. You should also decide whether you are doing anything to complicate the problem. Is the dog being left alone too much? Does it have enough toys to play with when left alone? Is it confined in a yard where other dogs are constantly passing and annoying or teasing it? Are you engaged in a general course of training that will give the dog a sense of purpose and accomplishment? Have you really gotten your meaning across to the dog? You should still teach your dog the meaning of the word, "quiet", but you should also make every effort to provide a situation where the dog will be comfortable and able to learn.

If you want your dog to bark sometimes, such as when someone comes to the door, you can teach it to bark at those times, even if you are teaching it "quiet" at other times. When the doorbell rings, jump, act nervous ("Who's that?"), look at the door ("Whozzat?"). When the dog barks, "Gooood dog!" If he won't quit when it turns out to be Uncle Harry at the door, "Quiet!" Give him lemon juice if needed. The dog will not be confused, if you are clear and consistent in your behavior. He will learn that barking is appropriate at some times, and not at others. Don't expect a young puppy to be protective of your home. You're supposed to protect him, and he knows it.

BITING: No puppy should ever be allowed to put its teeth on a human's skin. There are *no exceptions*. Tiny puppies are not allowed to chew on fingers; big dogs are not allowed to grab arms and legs, even in play. If you begin when your puppy is very young and help it get rid of any idea that it's O.K. to put its teeth on people, you will be laying a sound foundation for a happy, well-socialized life, free of lawsuits, sudden trips to the emergency room, and potential tragedy when your well-meaning but snappish dog is led away for the last time.

Every time your very small puppy chomps your finger say "OUCH!" but not the way a person would say it. Say it the way a puppy would say it—a high-pitched "YIPE!" Take your finger away. This is often all it takes. If the "YIPE!" doesn't seem to be working, try a sharp, "No!" and take your finger away *every time* the pup nips or chews. After correcting it, pet it and praise it immediately.

If talking to the puppy is obviously not working, smack it on the nose. Use only two fingers, and don't knock its head off, but give it a good sharp smack, and say "No!" This is the *only* time you should ever hit your puppy. Make friends again at once!

If you picked a puppy which is highly aggressive, smacking it on the snout is not going to work either. You should have paid attention to the chapter on picking a puppy—but we will assume you have your reasons for keeping the very aggressive pup. A tough cookie like this is going to view slaps as challenges. It will be nip, slap, nip, slap, nip, slap. Each slap will just reinforce his aggression.

Rub Bitter Apple all over your hands and forearms. When it nips, say "NO!" and pet it at once, as it foams at the mouth and wonders why you taste so bad. If this doesn't work, you need to have a talk with a good, responsible dog trainer. Stay away from the people who only take dogs six months or older, and look out for tough-guy dog trainers. Your very aggressive pup doesn't need a very aggressive trainer; the opposite is probably best.

BITING AND YOUNG CHILDREN: Exercise control in situations where there is a puppy, a new bone or bowl of food, and a very young child. This combination often leads to a nip. When it happens, smack the dog, put a bandaid on the child, forgive them both, and make it clear to the child that this is apt to happen again. It is up to the child to see that it doesn't. Don't make a big production of this event, either with the child or the dog; neither one of them is going to be permanently scarred unless you magnify the situation. Get the dog used to having someone put a hand in his food bowl when he is eating and take bones and food away from him. Start early and save wear and tear on your skin. Protect the puppy from nervous-making distractions when he is eating, but don't create an aura of sacred privacy. You will have to be able to remove things from his mouth at times when he picks up strange objects, like moldy doorknobs.

If you have raised an older dog with a biting habit, remember whose fault it is. Contact a professional dog trainer.

"Protection Training" is stupid, cruel, and dangerous. If you think you'd like to own a "protection trained" dog, either 1) you don't really know what that is, or 2) you are a very unpleasant person, and we will thank you to stop reading our book. The U.S. Army has statistics on the number of adult attack dogs which turn on their handlers between the ages of three and five years. Most responsible trainers agree that *all* attack or "protection" trained dogs constitute a serious threat to their owners, families, and innocent strangers. There is no reason on earth to have one. It is like wishing for your very own atomic bomb—you may be around when it happens to go off.

Teaching your dog not to bite does not mean that it will not protect you if you are in danger. It does mean that it will not be a threat to you, your family, and friends, and innocent people. A dog bite is no joke. Every year people are killed by dogs—in some cases by "totally reliable" protection dogs. There's no such thing. You've been warned. Anyone who tells you different is not your friend.

CHRONIC PIDDLING: Piddling (urinating a little bit) when being petted is a nervous habit some dogs develop. Young puppies sometimes have this problem because excitement makes them lose the little bladder control they have. If you notice that your puppy is getting older (three months and up) and is still piddling when it is greeted, you have a problem to solve. First check with your vet. A slight urinary tract infection sometimes causes this lack of control. If your pup is healthy, here's how you can help it.

Usually the pup or nervous adult dog will piddle when a family member or guest arrives at the door. If punished, or even scolded, such an animal will just piddle more. To cure this problem, stop giving the pup a big greeting upon arrival. Enter the house calmly, say hello softly, don't stoop to pet the pup (many piddlers sit when being petted, and piddle while they are sitting). Don't let guests fuss over the pup. Give the pup a chance to calm down. If you have been away for a while, leash the pup and take it outside to relieve itself the moment you get home.

MASTURBATION: Some people are worried by a puppy's habit of masturbating (mounting or humping) people's legs. This is a form of instinctive sex-play/dominance. Tell the puppy "No" and push him away every time. If an adult dog tries to masturbate on people's legs, furniture, rugs, etc., the best solution is probably to have him castrated. This will relieve his frustration and will usually eliminate his annoying social habit.

RUNNING IN TRAFFIC: One of the three basic *musts*, this is very simple. *Never* give the dog an opportunity to run in traffic. He should be leashed at all times until *very* securely obedience trained.

BOARDING YOUR DOG: It may be necessary for you to leave your dog overnight at the vet's or at a boarding kennel for a number of days or weeks. Check the place out, using the same standards as outlined for breeding kennels. Try to visit the boarding kennel with your dog the day before you plan to leave. Put him in one of the runs, and go away for a half-hour. When you return, play with him, take a walk with him, and leave him a second time. This way you have established a pattern of your return, and the separation will be much easier for your dog.

Don't let this long list of problems intimidate you. While we have met dogs who have every bad habit listed in this chapter, plus a few more, a well-chosen puppy, whose human family likes it and has expectations of pleasure and easy training, will not be a terrible headache in this department. Some people enjoy unraveling complicated dog problems (we do), but it is not a necessary part of dog owning. The best way to avoid serious behavior problems is to get a puppy less apt to cause them—and you know how to do that. The next step in problem prevention on a grand scale is to have a clear idea of what you want the puppy to become, have a well-worked-out plan for the first days and weeks the puppy will be at home, and a sense of humor and patience.

We won't speculate as to why this is, but those clients of ours who tend to get into a terribly wrought-up state of mind when their puppy shows signs of anti-social or problem behavior have puppies that get into a lot of trouble. Those clients who have an idea that the puppy will be more pleasure than trouble, and assume that any bad habits are a very temporary thing, have easy puppies, ones that get over bad habits very quickly or never get into any. There are breeds which seem to be more trouble than others, such as Alaskan Malamutes. It is your responsibility to find out enough about a given breed *before you bring one home* to be prepared for educating it.

14. BASIC OBEDIENCE AND BEYOND

There are levels of training beyond what a young puppy can learn from Chapter 12. In fact, your dog can continue to learn more demanding and complicated things all his life, if you and the dog enjoy that sort of thing. You may even like training and working with your dog so much that you will become interested in the sport of "obedience." There are obedience trials, often held in conjunction with dog shows in which you can compete. There are strict rules, and both dog and handler must work in a very precise manner to get a passing score (170 out of a possible 200 points in Novice Obedience). The only thing we don't like about A.K.C. Obedience competition is that no mixed-breed dogs are allowed to compete. You can find books which outline courses of training for the various levels of A.K.C. Obedience, and the A.K.C. will send you a free rule book.

Most people start out to obedience train their dogs by reading a book. This isn't a bad way to start, but it often doesn't work. The exercises make great sense when you read about them, but they don't seem to work out when you try them. We have done our best to limit this book to discussing things that can be learned from a book.

We will give you some basics about formal training, but it is like try-ing to teach someone how to ride a bicycle from a book. It goes much quicker and easier if there is someone on hand to *show* you just how it is done and then stand by to show you again, after you've tried it a couple of times. By all means, read a couple of training books by different authors, and get an idea of different approaches. Try out a few training exercises, but don't conclude that your dog is a bone head (or that you are) if the results are less than sparkling.

If book learning isn't the best way to get started in obedience training, then what? Obviously, someone who knows the ropes will have to show you how. Unless your next-door neighbor is an experi-enced dog handler, you are going to have to seek someone who has set up publicly to give or sell instruction.

A standard course in basic obedience will include these exercises:

Heel   The dog walks by your left side and sits when you stop.
Sit   The dog sits on command
Down   The dog lies down on command
Recall   The dog comes when called, sits in front of the handler.
Stand   The dog stands in one place
Finish   The dog takes the heel position from sitting in front, while the handler is standing still.
Stay   The dog stays put, while sitting, while lying down, while standing.

If your dog can do these things, but only when he is in the mood, you've made progress, but he still isn't obedience trained. Now, who will teach you these simple exercises? We will, of course, but not everyone who reads this book will be able to come to our school. Our local telephone directory lists twenty-three commercial dog schools. There are private dog trainers who advertise in newspapers and leave their cards in pet shops and vet's offices. There are classes in YMCAs, schools, lodge halls, and other meeting places. You can pay anywhere from twenty-five dollars to well over three hundred dollars to learn those few exercises.

It should be carefully noted that what you pay has *nothing* to do with what you get. Some of the twenty-five dollar courses couldn't be better, and some of the three hundred dollar courses couldn't be worse! What makes a dog training course good or bad? Results for one thing. Also the degree of competence and independence you,

Heel

Sit

Down

Recall

Finish

Stay

Basic Obedience Routine

the client, can come away with. And of course, humane and friendly methods. You don't want to make a nervous wreck out of the puppy you've lavished so much care on.

Anybody can open up a dog school. In most localities there are no requirements; you are a dog trainer if you say you are. There are plenty of unethical and ignorant people selling dog lessons. They are out for a fast buck, and charge accordingly (but not every expensive training course is a fraud). Style is something people pay for, and dog education might be divided into Deluxe, Standard, and Economy categories. Same training, different trappings.

THE DELUXE CATEGORY: The Deluxe category comes in two forms. *Mode One:* Your dog is sent away "for as long as it takes" (usually two weeks), often to the school's beautiful country estate (which you will never see). He comes back (they promise) fully trained, tail wagging, after a vacation his owners could envy (and afford if they hadn't sent *him*). Anyone who would risk his dog by sending him off to be trained or brutalized—you aren't there, and you can't know which—almost deserves the misery that schools of this kind often cause. Prices range from $250 to $750.

DELUXE CATERORY *Mode Two:* At least this way, you'll be the only one to take a beating. A trainer comes to your home "because the dog must be educated in his own environment—after all, Freud says that problems begin within the family, and within the family is the place to solve them." As far as we know Freud didn't say anything about dogs; they work differently than humans. The "we establish a dialogue with your pet" psychiatric school of dog training is just a way to take advantage of people who don't understand that dogs are not little human beings. The trainers are well spoken and educated, and they charge what a psychiatrist would charge, if a psychiatrist made house calls. There are some good trainers that make housecalls, and it is a better idea than sending the dog away to boarding school if you can't leave your house. Prices average about $45 an hour.

THE STANDARD CATEGORY: If you feel that you will learn better in a private lesson, as opposed to a class situation, this is the reasonable way. You and your dog go to the trainer once a week. The trainer teaches *you* to train your dog. If you have a difficult dog (very timid, bigger than you, clownish, nippy) this might be the best way. Some trainers begin with private lessons and then send their clients on to obedience clubs for class work. Prices range from $95 to $250.

THE ECONOMY CATEGORY: Group classes are held weekly, usually in some public facility, such as a YMCA. These classes offer you a chance to train your dog in distracting surroundings. Distractions are good—if you can get your dog to perform well with fifteen other dogs around, you're making good progress. It is the cheapest way, twenty-five dollars and up for a course lasting six to nine weeks. Some of the people who conduct these classes are dedicated hobbyists. They live and breathe dog training, and you can learn a lot from them. Maybe some of the instructor's enthusiasm will rub off on you, and you will discover that you've found a wonderful new hobby.

Look for an obedience instructor who belongs to the National Association of Dog Obedience Instructors. This is an organization of dog trainers who are generally expert and ethical. They will honestly try to teach you all they know. For the address of the current secretary of NADOI see *Off-Lead Magazine* (see Names and Addresses).

One problem about the Economy category is that the classes are not as easy to find as professional trainers. They're out there, but usually don't have much of an advertising budget. Call local kennel clubs, humane societies, and veterinarians to find a class in your area. The A.K.C. (see Names and Addresses) can supply lists of obedience clubs by state.

An excellent way to find out about what is offered in your area in the way of obedience classes is to go to a local match show. Check the papers to see if there is a "fun match" scheduled nearby with obedience events. Matches are practice gatherings for people who are preparing for sanctioned dogs shows and obedience trials. There are competitions, ribbons, and prizes, but it doesn't count toward obedience degrees, or titles. People are usually relaxed at fun matches, and you will have lots of chances to ask questions. Watch the people and dogs competing in the Obedience events. If you see someone whose dog has worked well, walk up and ask where they trained. Most people who go in for the sport of Obedience are friendly and anxious to pass information along. And don't just watch the Novice Obedience; have a look at the people and dogs working in Open and Utility classes—Rin Tin Tin stuff. If they seem to be having a lot of fun, it's because they are. Take a good look; it might be you in that ring someday.

Now that we've told you that books that attempt to tell how to teach formal obedience seldom help we will attempt to tell you how to teach your dog formal obedience. If you've got a willing puppy, and you've practiced the lessons in Chapter 12, you ought to make some progress. Don't get the idea that training stops here. Have a look at some books specifically about obedience training, try to visit an obedience trial or fun match to see experienced handlers at work, and consider enrolling in a training class. This chapter just shows a few basic approaches to the first stage of training.

The exercises in Obedience Training are much the same as the ones you learned in Chapter 12, with one big difference: A kindergarten puppy only has to do these things in a general way. If the dog is obeying commands more than half the time, you've done a good job. Now we are going to work with something close to perfection as our goal—we want the dog to respond to our commands 100 percent of the time.

A puppy is ready for Obedience Training when it is about four and one half to five months old. If your puppy did spectacular work in Puppy Kindergarten, and seems to be eager for more, you can start a little earlier. If you've got a big, rough, tough puppy that acted as though kindergarten was nothing but a joke, you might want to start formal training early for him, too. If your puppy is shy and retiring, or nervous, you might want to extend Puppy Kindergarten, and start on Obedience Training later, when he has more confidence. You know your puppy, and you have to decide when he's ready to leave kindergarten and start in first grade.

EQUIPMENT: You will need a flat leash made of leather or webbing (not chain!) about six feet long, a fifteen foot length of sash cord or clothesline with a clip on one end (you can get them in most hardware stores) and a training collar. There are various kinds of training collars: You've probably seen dogs wearing collars made of chain (like a noose) with a ring on each end. Some people call these

Correct way to put on chain collar

"choke collars", and used in the wrong way that's just what they are. We use them in the right way, and call them "training collars." They are *not* for choking! Training collars can be dangerous, and there are some rules about their use:

1. Never leave the chain collar on the dog when he is unsupervised. Dogs can catch one ring on a nail or other protrusion and strangle themselves.

2. Never tie the dog up using the chain collar. If you have to tie him, and the chain collar is the only one you have, attach the leash clip to the "dead" ring so the collar can't tighten.

3. Always keep the chain collar attached to the leash rather than the dog. This way you won't make a mistake and leave it on him.

4. Never keep metal tags or anything else attached to the chain collar. They can hurt the dog when the collar is tightened.

5. Always put the collar on the dog in the correct way, with the ring the leash attaches to passing through the "dead" ring to the right. When the collar is on the dog correctly, it will loosen by itself when you pull it tight and then release it. Try it on your wrist; if it stays tight, it's backwards.

Other types of collars are "chokes" made of nylon suitable for breeds with long silky hair that might get caught up in the links of a chain, and a sort of collar with pairs of blunt nasty-looking prongs all around the inside. We don't like the nylon collar when we can avoid using it, because it has little weight, and doesn't fall open as readily as the chain (some trainers prefer it). The blunt prong or finger collar is not as nasty as it looks, but it is a cumbersome thing that tangles in fur. There is also a collar on the market that looks nasty and really is, a leather collar with rows of sharp nails on the inside. If you find one for sale, call the Humane Society, or ASPCA, and they will have a talk with the man in the store.

The purpose of a training collar is to tighten suddenly around the dog's neck when you give the leash a sharp jerk. The purpose of this is to 1) get the dog's attention and 2) persuade him to do what you're telling him. This may sound cruel, but it really isn't. For one thing, a dog's neck is built differently from ours, and what would give us a neckache that would last all day is just uncomfortable enough to make a dog pay attention. It is something like being led around by the ear; it isn't exactly the most painful thing in the world, but you aren't inclined to resist if you see the person leading you is serious enough to pull your ear off. Your dog may yelp when you give him a correction, but it is his dignity that has been injured, not his neck.

It is possible to overdo the corrections with the training collar, but our experience has been that ninety-nine out of a hundred students have a tendency to underdo it. Of course, we'd much prefer that you find an experienced person to help you at this stage. Every dog needs a different correction, and a professional trainer can save you from having to experiment on your puppy.

Much more important than corrections with the leash and collar is praise. Praise your dog every time he gets anywhere near being right, and praise him after each jerk on the leash. The purpose of the leash and collar is not to punish but to correct; reassure him after every correction.

The best way to give you an idea of how to use the leash and collar is to demonstrate it. Since we can't be with you to demonstrate, we will just describe the exercises:

HEEL: The dog is sitting at your left side. The training collar is on properly, like a "P" lying on its back (ꊸ), the bottom of the "P"

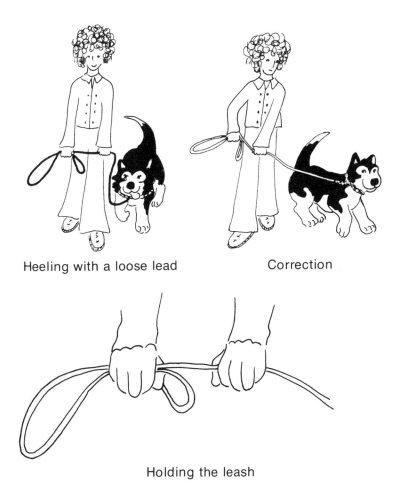

Heeling with a loose lead   Correction

Holding the leash

towards you (check this every time you practice). In a cheery voice, give the command, "Brutus, heel!" and step off with your left foot. Walk briskly. If the dog does not come with you, jerk the leash, slap your leg and encourage him, "That's a good boy, Brutus, heel!" Now you are both moving. If Brutus lags behind, jerk, "Come on Brutus, attaboy, heel!" If Brutus wanders off to the side, JERK! "Atsagoodboy, Brutus, heel!" Keep talking to him. If Brutus gets ahead of you, turn around and go the other way, fast! Jerk! "Gooood boy, Brutus heel!" After a while, Brutus is going to get the idea that you have suddenly become very clumsy and unreliable. He has to keep an eye on you every moment, because if his attention wanders you are going to go off in another direction and jerk that stupid leash.

And for some strange reason, the only place he is safe from those annoying corrections is walking by your left leg. You're obviously not mad at him, you've been speaking very pleasantly to him the whole time. Brutus will just decide that you're simple minded, and the best policy is to watch you carefully, and walk by your left leg whenever you start with this "Heel!" stuff. Congratulations, you've trained your dog to heel.

SIT: Brutus already knows this from kindergarten. What he does not know is that whenever you come to a stop, he is supposed to sit next to you. When you stop, don't stop on a dime. Slow down for a couple of steps first, and gently tighten the leash, *which must be loose at all times except when you're using it to tell the dog something!* After you stop, count two and then say, "Brutus, sit!" and jerk, straight up. If he doesn't sit, "Brutus sit!" and jerk, straight up. If he still doesn't do it, correct him again—this time reach down and touch his hindquarters to remind him of what he learned in kindergarten. After a while, the sitting when you stop becomes automatic, just count two in your head, and then jerk! straight up. After he is sitting, "Good boy!"

You can practice the heel and sit exercises together. Keep your practice sessions down to fifteen minutes a day. If the dog seems to really enjoy the lessons, you may give him two fifteen minute sessions, but beware of boring him! Once a dog gets bored with his training, you're in trouble. Make sure the dog has had a chance to eliminate before the lesson, and always end the lesson with a period of play and a little stroll.

STAY: Teach stay the same way you taught it in kindergarten, but extend the time to one minute at least for the sit-stay and stand-stay, and three minutes for the down-stay. Don't do more than three minutes on sit-stay and stand-stay. Beware of boredom and fatigue, keep the exercises pleasant for the puppy.

When teaching stay, always leave the dog a number of times, at various distances away from him, in succession. This is to keep him from anticipating a new command, and starting to move when you return.

STAND: Teach stand as it is given in Puppy Kindergarten.

Correction for Down

Correction for Sit

DOWN: Teach down as it is given in Puppy Kindergarten. Once you are sure the dog knows it, and is doing it most of the time, you can encourage him with a little tug on the leash, downwards, reaching under his chin. Try to work toward having the dog drop while you remain in a standing position.

RECALL: Teach the recall as it is given in Puppy Kindergarten. When you are sure the dog knows it, you can give little tugs on the leash to keep him coming straight, and to increase his speed. You may now start using the long piece of sash cord or clothesline for recalls over a longer distance. Don't get ahead of yourself and start to practice off-leash recalls, even if you're sure he can do it. It is better to wait until he is 100 percent perfect on the leash before ever starting to work off-leash. Concentrate on getting a straight sit in front of you at the end of the recall. Try not to use a correction here; a two-handed chin rub and a little gentle pressure may do the trick.

Teaching the Finish

FINISH: At the end of the recall, the dog is sitting directly in front of you. Now, take a big step backwards with your left leg, say, "Brutus heel!" and bring your leg forward again immediately. Guide the dog around so that he winds up in the heel position, sitting. "Gooood dog!"

We have just given you a very light dose of formal Obedience Training, because we believe it is better for you to find someone reliable to help you with this training. There are many techniques for teaching these exercises, and there are many types of dogs. It takes some experience to fit the right technique with the right dog. There isn't just one way to train that fits every dog, and trainers who think there is fail a lot. If you read a book in which the author says that his method is the only method and it works with every single dog in creation, you've either run up against a fool or a phoney. We will include a list of books about dog training at the end of this book. Don't read just one.

Whether you find a good trainer or class or club, or whether you rely on books, you have a good head start. Your puppy has been well chosen, well cared for, well nourished, and has had the advantage of Puppy Kindergarten. You will make mistakes in training—we all do—but your dog will be able to forgive you and start over. You can go as far as you like with training, make an Obedience competitor of your dog, or just a dog that's easy to live with. Whatever directions you take in training, we wish you the very best of luck.

15. HOW TO FIND A LOST DOG

These are some tips about finding a lost dog. Tip number one: Don't let him get lost in the first place. If your dog gets loose and wanders away, it is because some human wasn't smart enough to prevent it.

We hope you were smart enough to keep a collar (leather, not chain) with identification tags on your dog at all times. There's a good chance someone will find him and call you up.

Make sure someone is staying at home by the telephone while you are looking for the dog. Those identification tags won't do any good if there is nobody home to answer the phone. You may want to have identification numbers tattooed on your dog; there are a number of registration services that list dogs' tattoo numbers and inform owners if the dog is found. Ask your vet.

Make your search for the lost dog in a spiral route with home at the center. This is how dogs usually wander, going in ever-widening circles.

Ask people if they have seen the dog, especially children, who are apt to be more observant of such things. If you have a picture of the dog, take it along to show people.

Newspaper advertisments are good, but rather slow. By all means run an ad in the papers, but also see if a local radio station will broadcast a description of the dog. Try the local TV station too. Posting signs in store windows or in the window of your car will help too. There are fast-copy printing establishments all over the country, which can cheaply make any number of duplicates while you wait; a sheet with your phone number and a picture of the dog can be run off in a few minutes and handed around.

Listen for barking dogs as you search for your lost one. If there are confined dogs on his route, they are going to bark when they see yours running free.

If the dog has run away before, it is likely that he'll take the same route. Look for him where you found him last time. You may get to see the look of surprise on his face when he finds you waiting for him.

A hunter's trick for finding a lost dog in an unfamiliar area, such as woods, is this: If night is coming on, and there's no point in looking because you can't see anything, leave an article heavy with your scent (such as a coat) weighted down with a stone, and come back to the spot next morning. There's a good chance the dog will have back-tracked, found the coat, and will be sleeping next to it.

Angry as you may be, *don't* punish your dog after he has been found. Give him a warm welcome, and hope that he was scared enough while he was lost that he won't try it again. Figure out how he got loose, and make plans to prevent it in the future.

SOME SOURCES FOR
ADDITIONAL INFORMATION

NAMES AND ADDRESSES

SUPERPUPPY, 48 Bayberry Drive, Huntington, New York 11743
Superpuppy is the name of our school. If you have a training problem that is not covered in this book, a question about your dog, or just want to say hello, write us a letter (send a self-addressed, stamped envelope). If we can, we'll send you an answer.

AMERICAN DOG OWNERS ASSOCIATION, P. O. Box 746, Albany, N.Y. 12207
These are the people who worry about puppy mills, dog-fighting for sport, and other abuses. Their newsletter is pretty scary sometimes, but their work is important.

THE AMERICAN KENNEL CLUB, 51 Madison Avenue, New York, N.Y. 10010
The A.K.C. serves as a registry for most pure-bred dogs in this country. They can send you information about a number of things: breed clubs, rules for dog shows and obedience trials, and how to go about registering a pure-bred puppy. The A.K.C. maintains an information service to answer the questions of owners and potential owners of pure-bred dogs. They publish *The Complete Dog Book*, which contains pictures and breed histories, as well as information

about breeding, care and feeding of dogs. This is a good book to look at if you are at the "what breed do I want?" stage. A.K.C. also publishes a monthly magazine, *Pure Bred Dogs—American Kennel Gazette,* which contains news of various breed clubs, lists of dog shows and obedience trials all over the country, and the names and addresses of many breeders. A.K.C. is probably the single most valuable information source for dog owners. Make use of it—send for free booklets about the A.K.C. and its functions.

GAINES DOG RESEARCH CENTER, 250 North St., White Plains, N.Y. 10602

Gaines publishes several very useful booklets, almost all of which are free. Ask for a copy of *At Your Service,* which lists the booklets you can order. Gaines will send you booklets about first aid, feeding, training, a directory of hotels and motels that accept dogs, a terrific full-color chart of all recognized A.K.C. breeds, and lots of other useful stuff. Be sure to send them a card and get a copy of *At Your Service.*

PURINA PET CARE CENTER, Checkerboard Square, St. Louis, Mo. 63199

Purina also provides free booklets. Some good ones: *How To Enjoy A Dog Show* and *How To Enjoy an Obedience Trial.*

WAYNE DOG FOODS, Allied Mills, Inc., 110 N. Wacker Dr., Chicago, Ill. 60606

An excellent booklet: *Man's Best Friend.*

The largest publisher of dog books is HOWELL BOOK HOUSE, 730 Fifth Avenue, New York, N.Y. Ask for their current list.

If you want an out-of-print, or rare dog book write to FRIENDS OF MAN BOOKSHELF, 1030 Garden Street, Hoboken, N.J. 07030. If nobody else has it, this is the place to get it.

DOG WORLD MAGAZINE, 10060 West Roosevelt Rd., Chicago, Ill., 60153

Fairly interesting—a lot of ads, some from responsible breeders. But much of the material is of interest to breeders and exhibitors, rather than the average dog owner.

DOGS, 222 Park Avenue South, New York, N.Y.

A more generally interesting magazine with a variety of articles. Good photography.

OFF-LEAD, 8140 Coronado Lane, Rome, N.Y. 13440

If you are going to subscribe to a dog magazine, this is the one to get. It is all about training. Some of the articles are written for the professional dog obedience instructor, others are of general interest, some are about the latest scientific breakthroughs in dog psychology. Ask for a free sample copy.

There are a lot of magazines devoted to specific breeds or types of dogs. Some of these are published by the various breed clubs. You'll run across ads for some of them in the magazines mentioned above, and in the publications of whatever breed clubs you get hold of. It is a good idea to ask for a free sample copy of the newsletter or magazine whenever you write to a breed club for information. Most of the clubs have spares to send around.

Dog equipment and supplies can often be purchased cheaply through mail-order houses. Check dog magazines for these places, and write for their catalogs. A good quality nylon leash that sells for $8.50 in local pet shops can be ordered from a mail-order house for $4.00. One company we do business with is The Dog's Outfitter, Box 509, Glen Cove, N.Y. 11542. It is one company that sells Grannick's Bitter Apple.

To the best of our knowledge, the publications, organizations, and companies we recommend in this section are the same as advertised at the time of this writing, but please remember that things have a way of changing. A magazine can be first rate for years, get a new managing editor, and turn into an inaccurate, shabby piece of work in a month. We have the current list of breed clubs, but the job of corresponding secretary tends to move from person to person, and if we included names and addresses, half of them would probably be out of date by the time the book is printed. Do your own research, that way the results will be fresh.

A word of warning about dog magazines: Pets are a vast money-making industry in this country. Advertising is an exercise for the purpose of getting you to let go of your money. There are lots of fascinating gimmicks, special dog foods and supplements, books, and mail-order courses advertised in magazines. Some of them are good, and some of them are plain nonsense. Use your head. Just because an electric shock dog collar is advertised in a generally reputable magazine, don't get the idea that it is anything but a cruel and dangerous gimmick, and a waste of money besides. The same goes for breeders. Looking at this month's issue of a well-known dog magazine, we find ads from well-known ethical breeders right next to ads placed by notorious puppy farmers who are responsible for bringing grief into the lives of many innocent customers. The magazine can't check into every advertiser—it's up to you to be cautious.

SOME BOOKS

Here are some popular books. There are hundreds more. These are just a few books that we like, or think you'll have an easy time finding.

American Kennel Club, *The Complete Dog Book,* 11th ed. New York, Howell Book House, 1972.

Fox, Michael, *Understanding Your Dog.* New York, Coward, McCann & Geoghegan, Inc., 1972.

Johnson, Norman H., and Galina, Saul, *The Complete Puppy and Dog Book.* New York, Atheneum, 1965.

Lorenz, Konrad, *Man Meets Dog.* New York. Penguin Books, 1965

Mowat, Farley, *The Dog Who Wouldn't Be.* New York, Pyramid, 1970.

Pearsall, Milo, and Leedham, Charles, *Dog Obedience Training.* New York, Charles Scribner's Sons, 1958.

Pfaffenberger, Clarence, *The New Knowledge of Dog Behavior.* New York, Howell Book House Inc., 1971.

Saunders, Blanche, *Dog Training for Boys and Girls.* New York, Howell Book House Inc., 1971.

——, *How to Train, Groom, and Show Your Dog.* New York, Howell Book House Inc., 1972.

——, *Dog Care for Boys and Girls.* New York, Howell Book House, Inc., 1964.

Schuler, Elizabeth M., *Dog Owners' Answer Book*. New York, Simon & Schuster, 1976.

Strickland, Winifred, *Expert Obedience Training for Dogs*. New York, Macmillan, 1969.

Tossutti, Hans, *Companion Dog Training*. New York, Howell Book House Inc., 1964.

Vesey-Fitzgerald, Brian, *Dog Owners' Encyclopedia*. New York, British Book Center, 1972.

Way, Robert F., *Dog Anatomy*. Croton-on-Hudson, Dreenan Press, Ltd., 1974.

Whitney, Leon F., *Dog Psychology: The Basis of Dog Training*, 2nd ed. New York, Howell Book House, 1971.

SOME PARTING WORDS

In looking over lists of dog books, we find that a great many of them have the word "complete" in their titles. If any of them were complete, you wouldn't need the others. It is a common failing, especially among dog "experts" to think that one's own particular impressions and tendencies are petrified and eternal truth.

We don't think this book is "complete," it just scratches the surface. In writing it we learned how little we know about dogs, and how tiny this book is in comparison to the millions of words written about dogs in every language for thousands of years.

What we hope we have done in this book is suggest to you some possibilities and resources. We haven't found one method for raising and training dogs. Our method is to try to be thoughtful, find out as much as we can, and listen to what our instincts, and the dog's are trying to say. We hope you will like this method, and make whatever changes it needs to suit yourself.

We could never have written this book without the help of two idiotic middle-aged Alaskan malamutes who think they're still puppies, and who just a few minutes ago came galloping into this room in a state of great excitement. They had something to tell us that wouldn't wait. They jumped up and down, bashed into us, nuzzled and wagged. We reviewed all the things they could be asking for, and determined that all their physical comforts had been seen to. Besides, it wasn't that kind of excitement, it wasn't that kind of message. Then we realized. The window was open, and this is the first cold night of the fall. Winter will soon be here, and with it snow. It's nice of the dogs to point things like that out to us.

INDEX

The above photo is of Arnold, one of Jill and D. Manus Pinkwater's two Alaskan Malamutes. It was Arnold who led the Pinkwaters into the field of dog training.

The Pinkwaters bought Arnold from a less than honest puppy farmer. Arnold suffered from malnutrition and parasites, and he didn't smell very good either. Worse still was Arnold's habit of attacking any dog within his reach. And since Malamutes are very strong, the Pinkwaters decided to learn everything they could about dog care and training.

They took the flood of information on dog training methods and applied their own unique approach, adapting traditionally inflexible rules to Arnold's personality. Happily, their hard work paid off and Arnold calmed down—which eventually led to the opening of the Pinkwaters' dog school, "Superpuppy," and the writing of this book.